DAVE BARRY
is from *Mars*
and *Venus*

Also by Dave Barry

DAVE BARRY

is from *Mars* and *Venus*

DAVE BARRY

Crown Publishers, Inc. • New York

For my readers; bless their twisted little minds.

Grateful acknowledgment is made for permission to reprint the following copyrighted material: the *Miami Herald* for the photograph on page 73 and the *Asbury Park Press* for the excerpts on pages 195–96 from the article "Man Struck with Pasta Also Stabbed."

Special thanks to Bill Frakes for use of the photograph on page 270 and to the *Popular Music and Society* journal for use of the excerpts on pages 61–62 from the article "Air Ball: Spontaneous Large Group Precision Chanting."

Published by Crown Publishers, Inc., 201 East 50th Street, New York, New York 10022. Member of the Crown Publishing Group.

Random House, Inc. New York, Toronto, London, Sydney, Auckland
www.randomhouse.com

CROWN and colophon are trademarks of Crown Publishers, Inc.

All columns were previously published in *The Miami Herald.*

Printed in the United States of America

Design by Leonard Henderson

Library of Congress Cataloging-in-Publication Data
Barry, Dave.
  Dave Barry is from Mars and Venus / by Dave Barry.
  Collection of previously published columns.
  1. American wit and humor. I. Title.
PN6162.B2954   1997   814.'54—dc21   97–10698

ISBN 0-609-60066-4

10 9 8 7 6 5 4 3 2

Contents

This photo, from around 1952, shows me (*left*) with my sister, Kate, on a tricycle outside the house where we grew up in Armonk, New York. Between me and Kate is a child I do not recognize. So I'm just going to say it's Bill Clinton, and if he wants to deny it, let him sue.

Acknowledgments

I, alone, could never have produced this book. I say this mainly in case there are lawsuits. But also I want to give credit to the institutions and people whose help is invaluable to me, yet whose names never appear in my writing, unless of course they do something silly.

First, I thank my readers, a wondrously alert group of people who keep me posted on world events and who, every time I read my mail, remind me that I could not possibly make up a world weirder than the one I already inhabit.

I thank the *Miami Herald*, and particularly my editors at *Tropic Magazine*: Tom Shroder, Bill Rose, and John Barry, courageous journalists who do not hesitate to stand up for me when an angry reader calls the paper to complain about something I have written.

"He's not here," they say.

I thank Doris Mansour, *Tropic*'s office manager, a loyal friend who painstakingly proofreads my writing, which is no easy task because the Official Stylebook does not list spellings for words such as "bazootyhead."

I thank my editor at Crown, Betty A. Prashker, who's savvy and supportive, and who can make a person feel right at home even when she's taking the person to lunch at the Four Seasons, a New York City restaurant where the asparagus costs approximately $85 per spear.

I thank my agent, Al Hart, who is a rare combination—

wise *and* enthusiastic—and whose letters are always funnier than mine.

I thank my irreplaceable assistant and research department, Judi Smith, who can find out anything and talk to anybody, and who usually knows what I'm thinking, so I don't have to.

Above all, I thank my son, Rob, who's still willing to go out with me and help me test the world's most powerful head-mounted water gun, even though, unlike his dad, he's really gotten too mature for that kind of thing; and my wife, Michelle, who makes me endlessly happy *and* takes me to basketball games.

All these people helped make this book possible. But let me make one thing clear: If there are any errors or omissions in this book, these people are *not* responsible. In the end, there is only one person responsible for what I write, and that person, of course, is: Donald Trump. Thank you.

Introduction

First, a few words about the title.

It isn't easy, coming up with book titles. A lot of the really good ones are taken. *Thin Thighs in 30 Days,* for example. Also *The Bible.*

Another restriction was that the publisher wanted a title with my name in it. Over the years, most of my book titles have had my name in them (*Dave Barry Turns 40, Dave Barry Turns 41, Dave Barry Develops a Nasal Polyp,* etc.). I realize this sounds egotistical, but it's not my idea. I'd be a lot happier if the book titles had a name with more appeal to the mass public, like "Stephen King" or "The Beatles." If it wasn't for the potential legal hassles, this book would be called something like *Develop Washboard Abs in One Hour with John Grisham and Madonna (As Seen on Oprah).*

Anyway, the first title actually considered for this book was *Another Damn Dave Barry Book.* I liked that one, because it was punchy, yet at the same time it said absolutely nothing. But then Crown changed its mind and decided against this title, presumably on the grounds that the word "damn" would offend some people, who would therefore not buy the book. Of course you could argue that this was a good reason to *use* the title, because people who'd be offended by the word "damn" would probably suffer cerebral hemorrhages if they read the book's actual contents.

But *Another Damn Dave Barry Book* was definitely out. Instead, Crown wanted to use *Dave Barry Exposes Himself,* featuring a cover photo of me wearing only an overcoat, which I would be holding open to display my body, with my strategic parts covered by the title (insert your font-size joke here). After a certain amount of hemming and hawing, as well as faxing, I rejected this title. My argument was that the cover concept was a stale old sight gag, but the real reason was that I didn't want to expose my body. I do not have Washboard Abs; I have Stealth Abs, protected from detection by a strategic layer of radar-absorbing flab.

For a while my editor at Crown, Betty Prashker, tried to argue me into accepting *Dave Barry Exposes Himself.*

"The way we see it," she said, "every time you write something, you're exposing yourself."

This is the kind of thing editors can say, secure in the knowledge that *they* won't be appearing on a book cover wearing only an open overcoat.

But I was firm in my opposition. And thus began a spate of title brainstorming. My agent, Al Hart, came up with what I thought was a winner—*Dave Barry Wants to Chew Your Hair*—but Crown was not receptive. Crown also rejected one of mine that I thought beautifully captured the spirit not only of this book, but virtually my entire body of work: *Armpit Noises from the Heart.* I also had no luck with:

Who Are You Calling Immature?
By Dave "Booger" Barry

Here are some of the other titles that didn't make it:

While You Were Holding Down a Real Job,
Dave Barry Was Writing This

A Funny Title Goes Here

Dave Barry Lowers His Standards Even More

How to Remain Sophomoric in the Coming Millennium

This Book Is All True
And Other Lies by Dave Barry

This Book Has Nothing to Do with the O.J. Trial

Humor Writers Who Run with Wolves

The Wisdom of Dave Barry
Would Be a Really Short Book, So We Printed This One Instead

And of course:

Moby Dave

But none of these was acceptable to everybody. Finally, just when it was beginning to look as though we'd never come up with a title, and the book would never get published—which would be a tragedy for civilization—we agreed on *Dave Barry Is from Mars* and *Venus*. It combines the two most essential elements of a classic book title:

1. Nobody has any idea what it means.
2. I don't have to get naked for the cover.

In addition to a title, this book also has contents, and I'd like to say a few words about them. Mostly what you will find in this book are short essays on a wide variety of important topics that are of concern to the informed, concerned citizen, such as turkey rectums. Because of the breadth of topics I cover in my *oeuvre*,[1] people often ask me what methodology I use in my research and writing. Here it is:

1. After a hearty breakfast, I scan the *Miami Herald* and other major daily newspapers, looking for important news developments and making mental notes. ("Huh!" is my exact phrasing.)
2. Lunch.
3. I fire up my laptop computer and, after some thought, type out the subject, or "topic idea," of an essay, such as: "Robot cockroaches."
4. Nap.
5. I fire my laptop computer back up and start "fleshing out" my topic idea by developing possible themes for discussion and amplification ("Robot cockroaches—a bad idea?").
6. Lunch.
7. At this point, heeding the old maxim that "all work and no play makes Jack Nicholson try to kill his family with an ax," I generally knock off for the day, only to return the next day and start the whole "grind" all over again, taking a harshly critical look at my work output from the day before, revising and polishing it, not stopping until the words convey precisely the message that I have formulated in my mind's eye ("Robot cockroaches—a bad idea? Or what?").

1. Literally, "eggs."

Sometimes I also do field research. For example, in researching the essays in this book, I climbed a giant scary
tree in a beaver-infested area; experienced Total Brain
Lockup while competing on the TV show *Wheel of Fortune*;
played the role of a corpse in an opera in Eugene, Oregon;
got hit by a car; nearly drowned with the U.S. Synchronized
Swimming National Team; became the only person I know
of to be sent to the emergency room with a laser-tag injury;
threw up in an F-16 exceeding the speed of sound; and, of
course, set fire to my toilet.

I'm not trying to impress you; it's my *job* to do this kind
of research. I'm no different from other leading columnists
such as George Will or William Safire, both of whom set fire
to their toilets on virtually a daily basis.

Why do we do these things? I can't speak for Bill and
George, but as for myself, I do them because I believe—call
me an idealist if you want—that even in this incredibly
complex global society, one lone person, using only his
mind and the power of information, *can* make a difference.

And I definitely do *not* want that person to be me.

This is me, probably around age four, with a gun that shot Ping-Pong balls. I loved that gun and shot Ping-Pong balls at everything and everybody. Perhaps that is why I had no friends.

I AM NOW A
TRAINED EGGBEATER

ATLANTA—There's an old saying in journalism: "Be careful of what you make fun of, because you could find yourself upside down attempting a Vertical Split while your lungs rapidly fill with water."

There's a lot of truth in this saying, as I found out when I took the Synchronized Swimming Media Challenge.

Here's what happened: Ever since Synchronized Swimming became an official Olympic sport, we journalists have ridiculed it. The thrust of our gist is: "Exactly what is so athletically impressive about people swimming around in circles while smiling like recently escaped lunatics? ANYBODY could do that!"

Eventually the Synchronized Swimming community got tired of hearing this, and responded as follows: "Oh YEAH? Well how about if YOU try it, Expense Account Butt?"

And thus I found myself at Emory University, wearing nose clips and goggles, in a pool about the size of Lake Huron, only deeper, with a dozen young and extremely fit members of U.S. Synchronized Swimming National Team

One, who will basically be the U.S. Olympic Team for the 2000 Games in Sydney, Australia.

Also in the pool was my synchronized media partner and *Herald* colleague, sports columnist Dan Le Batard. Dan and I, knowing that the full masculine studliness of our bodies would be on display, had prepared for the challenge via a grueling fitness regimen of not having eaten a single Snickers bar for the entire previous hour. I estimate that our body fat content had plummeted to somewhere around 87 percent.

The spokesperson for U.S. Synchronized Swimming, Laura LaMarca, had told me earlier that we fit the basic profile of journalists who had taken the Challenge.

"Floating is definitely not a problem for the media," she said.

That may be true, but I was pleased to see that there were two lifeguards on hand.

"That's standard procedure," LaMarca said. "A one-to-one ratio of lifeguards to journalists."

The Kitchen Utensil Stroke

With our safety assured, Dan and I started learning our synchronized maneuvers. The first one was called Eggbeatering, which is when you move your legs around like an eggbeater, so you can keep your head and shoulders above the pool surface while you raise your arms gracefully into the air.

At least that's how it worked for the members of National Team One. When Dan and I gracefully raised OUR arms, our entire bodies, arms and all, immediately sank like anvils. So when we all tried the maneuver together, there was a circle of a dozen young women, smiling and raising their arms, and in the middle of the circle there was this bubbling, violently turbulent patch of water, underneath which were Dan and me, trying desperately to eggbeater our way back to the surface before our lungs exploded.

After we gave up on eggbeatering, we tried the Ballet Leg, which is when you lie on your back and raise your leg gracefully into the air. When the synchronized swimmers did this, their bodies remained absolutely steady and horizontal, they appeared to be lying on floats. When Dan and I attempted it, we hit the pool bottom so hard we left dents.

At this point I noticed that the lifeguards were standing much closer.

My favorite maneuver was the Vertical Split, which is when you get yourself upside down in the water, then do some kind of arm thing that causes you to shoot up, Polaris-like, so that your legs and hips come all the way out of the water, at which point you execute a graceful split. We attempted this as a group, with Dan and me again in the middle, and I will never forget the sight from the bottom of the pool, where I of course immediately found myself. All around me were the national team members, their bodies upside down and perfectly vertical, submerged only from head to waist, their legs high in the air; next to me, also on the bottom, was Dan, of the water.

That's the only maneuver you'd see, if the media ever did get a team together: Synchronized Toes.

Anyway, after about 45 straight minutes of alternately eggbeatering and sinking, I came to the surface, and, using what little air I had left in my lungs, shouted, "THIS IS THE HARDEST SPORT IN THE WORLD!"

Then, and only then, did they let us out of the pool.

THE AVENGING DEATH KILLER OF DOOM

I found out about laser tag from a guy I know named Woody. Woody is in public relations, despite the fact that he looks like—and I say this as a friend—a street person who has failed to take his medication since 1972. I believe this is the secret of his success: When Woody approaches business people, they expect him to ask them for spare change, and possibly throw up on their shoes, and when he doesn't, they're so relieved that they agree to let him handle their public relations.

Anyway, Woody represents this outfit that operates a laser-tag game, and he'd been bugging me to try it.

"It's really cool," he said. "Everybody runs around and tries to shoot everybody else."

"Woody," I said, "that doesn't sound like a *game*. That sounds like *Miami*."

But finally I decided to look into it, because I'm a journalist, and in my line of work, you never know when you're going to come across a socially significant new phenomenon, except that this will definitely not happen to you if you're playing laser tag.

And thus on a Friday afternoon I went with my son, Rob, to the laser-tag place, Q-Zar, in Coconut Grove, which is a part of Miami where busloads of European tourists go to enjoy the unique South Florida tropical experience of meeting and mingling with other European tourists, sometimes from completely different buses.

The laser-tag place was staffed by wholesome-looking young people. They collected $7.50 apiece from us and ushered us into the Briefing Room, along with about a dozen others who would be playing the game—some teenage boys, a family with munchkin-sized children, and two women who looked as though they came directly from work.

At this point we were just ordinary humans with no interest in killing each other.

A staff person divided us into a Red Team and a Green Team, then explained the principles of the game, which boil down to: Shoot the other team. (Actually, the staff person, for public-relations reasons, used the term "tag" instead of "shoot.") Each time you get shot you lose a life; after you lose four lives, you go to the Re-Energizer, where—here's a major improvement over reality—you get four MORE lives.

The staff person also said we could use our lasers to deactivate the Enemy Base.

"Why would we do that?" asked one of the women who looked as though they came directly from work.

Rob and I smirked at each other, guy-to-guy, trying to imagine the mental state of a person who would not immediately grasp the importance of deactivating the Enemy Base. Our smirks got even smirkier when this woman asked if it was okay to play the game *wearing high heels and carrying purses.*

Sometimes you have to wonder what is happening to this nation.

After the briefing, we went into the Vesting Room, where we each got a laser gun, attached to a red or green plastic vest (the vest has a device that vibrates when somebody shoots you). Then we were led to a big, dark, semi-spooky room with artificial smoke drifting around and a big maze in the middle, full of nooks and crannies where a person could skulk. The two teams went to opposite ends of the room. Then a voice on the loudspeaker said "5 . . . 4 . . . 3 . . . 2 . . . 1 . . ." and suddenly the room was filled with extremely loud pulsating music apparently created by musicians beating their amplifiers to death with rocks.

I am not a violent person. I am a product of the Flower Power sixties. I have actually worn bell-bottomed jeans and stood in a mass of hundreds of people, swaying back and forth, singing, 'Everybody get together, try to love one another right now,' having vivid visions of World Peace. (Granted, some of us were also having vivid visions of giant red frogs hopping across the sky, but that's another issue.) I haven't been in a fight since seventh grade and have never owned a gun.

But when the laser-tag game started, a primeval reptile instinct took over my brain, turning me instantly into The Avenging Death Killer of Doom. I made Rambo look like Mister Rogers. I was a wild man—darting through the dark maze, ducking around corners, making totally unintelligible combat-style hand signals to my teammates. At one point, I swear, I signaled to my son, and, without a trace of irony, yelled "Cover me!" My nervous system was on Maximum Overload Red Alert, because I knew that somewhere

22

out there, in that smoky gloom, was The Enemy, and I had to hunt him down without pity, because he was a merciless killer who would not hesitate to . . .

BZZZZZZZZZZ

NO! My vibrator is vibrating! I've been SHOT! The Enemy is even more deadly than I thought! He is vicious! He is brutal! He is . . .

He is a woman wearing high heels.

At least she didn't hit me with her purse.

I also got nailed repeatedly by the munchkins. The Avenging Death Killer of Doom spent a lot of time skittering back to the Re-Energizer, trailed by a persistent seven-year-old with excellent aim who was making The Avenging Death Killer of Doom's vest vibrate like a defective alarm clock.

But I also scored a few hits myself, and at one point—I want this in my obituary—I deactivated the Enemy Base. Overall I found the experience to be far more entertaining than anything currently being funded by the National Endowment for the Arts. And to those of you who feel that this kind of game is bad because it might encourage aggressive behavior in a society that is already far too violent, let me say that, while I understand your point, I also feel that this type of "play-acting" activity can provide a harmless release for aggressiveness and actually *reduce* violence. So shut up or I'll kill you.

LOSING FACE

Today's Topic Is: Living Smart

What do I mean by "Living Smart"? Let's look at a simple example:

Suppose that two people—call them Person A and Person B—are late for appointments in New York City and need to cross the street. Person A rushes into the street without looking; he is instantly struck by a taxi going 146 miles per hour (this taxi has engine trouble; otherwise it would be going much faster). But Person B—even though he's in an equally big hurry—pauses on the sidewalk and looks both ways. While doing this, he is severely beaten by muggers.

So we see that the choices we make affect the quality of our lives, and we must always try to make the smartest choice, which in this case would be the one made by Person C, who decided to skip his appointment and remain in his hotel room watching the movie *Laundromat Lust*.

I'll give you another example of "living smart," from my own personal life. On a recent Friday night, my son, Rob, and I were in Miami, playing laser tag, a game wherein you skulk around in a darkened maze, wearing a special electronic vest attached to a laser gun. The object is to shoot your opponent in his vest or gun, thereby scoring valuable points.

I was standing in the dark, with my back pressed against a wall, a few feet from a corner. I knew Rob was around that corner. Quickly, I ran through my options:

Option One: Run around the corner with my gun held out in front, thereby exposing it to Rob's laser fire.

Option Two: Protect my gun by holding it back and running around the corner with my face out in front.

Looking back on what happened, I realize that I should have gone with Option Three. "Find some activity more appropriate for a 49-year-old, such as backgammon."

Instead I went with Option Two, running around the corner face-first, which turned out to not be such a great idea, because Rob had gone with Option One, running around the corner gun-first.

The result was that my face, specifically my right eye socket, collided violently with Rob's gun. But at least he didn't score any valuable points!

After the collision, I lay on the floor for a while, moaning and writhing, but eventually I was able to get back on my feet, and in just a matter of seconds—the recuperative powers of the human body are amazing—I was back down moaning and writhing on the floor again.

"You need to go to the hospital," said Rob.

"Gnhnong," I said. "Gnhime gnhowaagh."

That was me attempting to say, "No, I'm okay." In fact, I didn't feel so hot, but in my experience, if you go to a hospital for any reason whatsoever, including to read the gas meter, they give you a tetanus shot.

So my plan was to tough it out. Leaning on Rob, I staggered out of the laser-tag place onto the sidewalk, where I had an excellent idea: Why not get down on all fours and throw up for a while? So I did. Nobody paid much attention; in Coconut Grove on a Friday night, it's unusual to see somebody NOT throwing up.

By this point Rob had gotten somebody to call a cab, and he insisted that we go to a hospital. When we got there I attempted to explain to a nurse what had happened; this was difficult because (a) I wasn't totally coherent, and (b) the nurse had never played laser tag.

"He shot you in the eye with a *laser*?" she said.

"Gnhnong," I said.

"Have you had a tetanus shot recently?" she said.

"YES!" I said, demonstrating the brain's amazing recuperative power to lie in an emergency.

They stuck some kind of needle in me anyway (hey, rules are rules). Then various doctors had a look at me, and, after a fair amount of peeking and probing, they determined that I had been hit in the face. They also told me I'd be okay.

And I'm sure I will, although at the moment part of my face is numb, and my right eyeball could pose for the cover of a Stephen King novel. Also I feel sleepy all the time. This made me a little nervous, so I did what medical experts recommend that you do whenever you have a question concerning your health: I called my friend Gene Weingarten, who is a professional newspaper editor and probably the world's leading hypochondriac.

Gene spent a day researching my symptoms and called back to tell me that, in his opinion, I have a condition known as "somnolence." "Somnolence" means, in layperson's terms, that you feel sleepy. Gene recommended that I get a CAT scan, but of course Gene would also recommend a CAT scan for earwax, so I went back to bed.

But forget about my personal medical problems. The point I'm trying to make is that, by considering your options and making the right decisions—"living smart"— you CAN lead a happy, healthy, and financially success- ful life. And if you do, please buy a bunch of groceries and have them delivered to me, because I really don't feel like going out.

WEIGHT LOSS THROUGH ANTI-GRAVITY

I am pleased to report that we finally have a scientific explanation for why everybody in the world is gaining weight. At least I am, and I know it's not my fault. Granted, I do not have the best dietary habits. Sometimes in a restaurant I will order fried, fatty foods ("Give me a plate of fried, fatty foods, and hurry" are my exact words). But I compensate for this by engaging in a strict exercise regimen of vigorously pounding the bottom of the ketchup bottle for as long as necessary. "No pain, no gain," that is my motto regarding ketchup.

Nevertheless, I have been gaining weight, and you probably have, too, which is why you're going to be happy to learn that neither of us is responsible. The universe is responsible. We know this thanks to a scientific insight that was had by alert fourteen-year-old Massachusetts reader Tim Wing. Tim reports that he was browsing through *The Osborne Book of Facts and Lists* when he came across the following fact: Every single day, including federal holidays,

25 tons of space dust lands on the Earth. This means that every day, the Earth weighs 25 tons more, which means that it contains a larger quantity of gravity, which as you know is the force made up of invisible rays that cause all physical objects in the universe to become more attracted to bathroom scales.

What this means, Tim Wing points out, is that "without gaining an ounce, people all over the world are getting heavier."

And there is more bad news: At the same time that gravity is increasing, the entire universe is expanding, except for pants. Pants are staying the same size, which means that—and this has been confirmed by extensive scientific tests conducted in my home—a "33-inch waist" pant will barely contain a volume that formerly fit easily into a 31-inch-waist pant. Albert Einstein accurately predicted this phenomenon in 1923 when he formulated his Theory of Pants Relativity, which also states, as a corollary, that as the universe grows older, "It will get harder and harder to find anything good on the radio."

But our big problem is this gravity buildup, which has already started to pose a grave threat to public safety. I refer here to an incident that occurred recently in Fort Lauderdale, Florida, where, according to a September 16 *Miami Herald* story that I am not making up, "A loggerhead turtle fell from the sky and hit a man in his white Chevy Nova."

(SCENE: The hospital emergency room)
    Doctor: *Where was the victim hit?*
    Nurse: *In his Chevy Nova.*
    Doctor: *Okay, let's do a CAT scan, and I want his oil changed immediately.*

Seriously, the man was unhurt, and so was the turtle, which, according to the *Herald* story, was apparently dropped by a seagull. But that is exactly my point: Since when do seagulls—one of the most sure-handed species of bird—drop turtles? The obvious answer is: *Since turtles started getting heavier,* along with everything else.

And as space dust continues to land on Earth, the situation will only worsen, with chilling results. According to my calculations, at the current rate of gravity buildup, by the year 2038, an ordinary golf ball will weigh the equivalent, in today's pounds, of Rush Limbaugh. Even a professional golfer, using graphite clubs, would need dozens of strokes to make such a ball move a single foot. An average round of golf would take four months—nearly *twice* as long as today.

Is that the kind of world we want our children to grow up and develop gum disease in? I think not. This is why we must call upon the scientific community to stop puttering around with global warming and immediately develop a solution to the gravity problem.

(30-second pause)

Well, we see that the scientific community has once again let the human race down, leaving it up to us civilians to deal with the situation. Fortunately, I have come up with a practical answer in the form of a:

Gravity Reduction Plan

Follow my reasoning: The problem is that 25 tons of stuff is landing on the Earth every day, right? So the obvious solution is to put 25 tons worth of stuff into a rocket every day and blast it into space. It couldn't be simpler!

Perhaps you're saying: "But, Dave, how are we going to find 25 tons worth of stuff every single day that is so totally useless that we can just send it into space with total confidence that it could never possibly in any way benefit humanity?"

I can answer that question in three simple words: "Fourth Class Mail." Every day at *least* 25 tons of this material is painstakingly mailed all over the United States and thrown away immediately upon receipt. Solid-waste experts estimate that 78 percent of our nation's landfill capacity is currently occupied by sincere unopened letters from Ed McMahon informing people that they have almost definitely won $14 million. Why not just load this material directly into rockets? And consider this: If we send up MORE than 25 tons a day, the Earth would actually LOSE gravity. I calculate that every human being on the planet would instantly be six ounces lighter if we also sent Ed up there, not that I am necessarily proposing this.

So I say let's fire up the rockets and get this program going before gravity gets so strong that all we can do is lie on the ground, helpless, while turtles rain down upon us. If you agree, write to your senators and congresspersons today and let them know where you stand. Stress the urgency of the situation. Stress their responsibility as public officials. Above all, stress that there's room in the rocket with Ed.

This certificate proves that I was confirmed at St. Stephen's Episcopal Church on December 18, 1960. The church evidently had much lower standards in those days.

THE HOT SEAT

If you were to ask me how I came to set my toilet on fire, I would answer you in two simple words: *Reader's Digest*.

I am referring specifically to the February 1995 issue of *Reader's Digest*, which was sent to me by alert reader Jeff Jerrell, who had spotted a startling article originally written for *Health* magazine by Mary Roach.

The article is about germs, which are extremely tiny organisms—many of them smaller than the artist formerly known as Prince—that can be found in huge quantities virtually everywhere. To get an idea of what I mean, conduct the following:

Scientific Germ Experiment

Get a microscope and some spit. Put the spit on a glass slide and put it under the microscope lens. Now look through the eyepiece. You'll notice, if you look closely, that you can't see anything, because you have no idea how to operate a microscope. But while you're looking, billions of germs, left on the eyepiece by the previous microscope user, will swarm into your eyeball—which to them is a regular Club Med—

and start reproducing like crazy via wild bacterial sex. You'll probably need surgery.

Getting back to *Reader's Digest*: The February article concerns leading University of Arizona germ scientist Chuck Gerba, Ph.D., who is a serious student of bacteria found in bathrooms. Consider the following absolutely true facts:

1. He routinely goes into public rest rooms, unarmed, and takes bacteria samples from the toilets.
2. His son's middle name is "Escherichia," after *Escherichia coli*, also known as *E. coli*, which is a common type of fecal bacteria.

Needless to say I had to call this man.

"You named your son after *bacteria*?" was my opening question.

"He finds that it's a good conversation starter," Gerba replied. "If we'd had a girl, we were going to name her 'Sally Salmonella.' "

Gerba told me that there are definite hazards associated with his line of study.

"When you spend a lot of time taking samples on your knees in the stalls of public rest rooms," he said, "people tend to call the cops on you. I've had to do some fast talking. I tell the cops, 'It's okay! I'm a scientist!' And they say, 'Yeah, right, we arrested a couple of scientists in this stall just last night.' "

Gerba told me that, in the course of his studies, he has learned some Amazing Toilet Facts:

Toilet Fact No. 1—Based on scientific measurements of the holes in public-toilet seats, "Americans have the biggest butts in the world."

Toilet Fact No. 2—In any group of public toilets, the first stall is likely to have the least bacteria, and the middle ones are likely to have the most, because more people use them. (In determining the rate of usage, Gerba went into public toilets and *numbered the toilet paper squares*.)

Toilet Fact No. 3—The cleanest public toilets are found in national-chain restaurants; the worst are found in gas stations.

"I'm surprised," Gerba said, "that no new life form has ever evolved from a gas-station toilet."

Toilet Fact No. 4—Every toilet user leaves a unique bacterial pattern; we know this thanks to a breakthrough technique Gerba developed called (I am not making any of this up) the Commode-A-Graph.

"If there's ever a crime committed on a toilet," Gerba said, "I can tell you who did it."

(Asked if this technique could be a factor in the O.J. Simpson trial, Gerba replied, "Not unless he washed his hands in the toilet.")

Toilet Fact No. 5—When you flush, a process called "aerosolization" takes place, in which the toilet shoots out an invisible cloud of tiny, germ-infested water droplets that get all over everything. In *Reader's Digest*, author Roach quotes Gerba as saying that if you keep your toothbrush within six feet of a commode, "you're basically brushing your teeth with toilet water."

So we see that a toilet is really nothing more than—to use a scientific parlance—a Yuck Bomb. The question is, what can you do about it? Is there any way to get a toilet *really* clean? This brings us to the truly fascinating part of Roach's article, wherein Gerba and his family, demonstrating the only way to kill all the bacteria, put laboratory alcohol on their commode bowl and—this is right on page 64 of *Reader's Digest*, if you don't believe me—set it on fire.

Let me stress right here that Gerba is a recognized toilet expert, and he had a fire extinguisher ready, and toilet-torching is VERY dangerous. You, the layperson, would be an irresponsible idiot to try it.

Fortunately, I am not a layperson; I am a trained humor columnist, and if there's one thing I enjoy, it's a clean toilet. So I tried Gerba's technique, and I have to say that, in a darkened room, a flaming toilet has a strange kind of beauty that can only be described as "a strange kind of beauty."

I'm tempted to speculate here on whether it might be possible to use this same technique to kill bacteria on other surfaces, such as the bodies of Tobacco Institute scientists, but I think I'm already in enough trouble as it is. So let me leave you with these important Toilet Health Reminders: (1) Avoid those middle stalls; (2) Move that toothbrush; and above all, (3) Don't sit down until the bowl has completely cooled.

THE PILGRIMS WERE TURKEYS

Thanksgiving is a time of traditions, and there is no tradition more meaningful than the annual U.S. Department of Agriculture warning about fatal food-dwelling bacteria.

This year, I'm pleased to report, the department has outdone itself: For the first time ever, the department has officially advised Americans *not to stuff their turkeys*. Many alert readers sent in an Associated Press item in which the acting director of the Agriculture Department's Meat and Poultry Hot Line—whose name is (I am not making any of this up) Bessie Berry—is quoted as saying: "Improperly cooked stuffing can cause serious illness or even death."

I am frankly wondering if stuffing should be regulated, like assault rifles, to prevent it from falling into the wrong hands.

Bank Teller: May I help you?
Robber: Hand over the money!
Second Bank Teller: Do as he says! He's holding improperly cooked stuffing!

But the looming specter of a painful death should in no way dampen the festivity of your Thanksgiving dinner. Just make sure the food is prepared in accordance with federal guidelines ("STEP ONE: Lighting the Blowtorch"). And before you eat, don't forget to bow your head for the traditional prayer of thanks ("We thank Thee for this bountiful meal and ask Thine forgiveness for the fact that we hath ordered pizza").

Another traditional thing you should do is teach your kids the true meaning of Thanksgiving. I suggest you have them put on the following historical play, *The Very First Thanksgiving*, which I wrote myself after several backbreaking minutes of research in the encyclopedia.

The Very First Thanksgiving

(*SCENE ONE: Some Pilgrims are standing on the deck of* the **Mayflower.**)

> **First Pilgrim:** *Well, here it is, the year 1620.*
>
> **Second Pilgrim:** *Yes, and we have been on this tiny ship, the* Mayflower, *for many weeks, fleeing persecution in England because of our religious views.*
>
> **Fourth Pilgrim:** *Also, we wear hats that look like traffic cones.*
>
> **First Pilgrim:** *What happened to the Third Pilgrim?*
>
> **Second Pilgrim:** *He's throwing up.*
>
> **Fourth Pilgrim:** *Hey, look! There's Plymouth Rock! Pull over, captain!*
>
> **Long John Silver:** *Arr.*

(*SCENE TWO: The Pilgrims are standing on the shore.*)

First Pilgrim: *Well, this looks like a barren area with poor soil and harsh winters, offering little chance for our survival.*

Other Pilgrims: *Perfect!*

Robber: *Hand over the money!*

First Pilgrim: *Hey! You already did your scene in this column!*

Robber: *Whoops.*

Second Pilgrim: *Look! A Native American!*

Native American: *Fortunately, I speak English. My name is Squanto.*

Fourth Pilgrim: *"Squanto"? What kind of name is "Squanto"?*

Second Pilgrim: *It sounds nasty! It sounds like, "Mom! The dog made Squanto on the linoleum!"*

First Pilgrim: *What's "linoleum"?*

Second Pilgrim: *I have no idea.*

Squanto: *I'm going to show you how to plant maize and beans using alewives, shad, or menhaden as fertilizer.*

Fourth Pilgrim: *"Alewives"?*

Squanto: *That's what it says in the encyclopedia.*

(SCENE THREE: One year later.)

First Pilgrim: *Well, here it is, one year later.*

Second Pilgrim: *That was a pretty harsh winter.*

Fourth Pilgrim: *That was definitely the last winter I plan to spend in a small confined space with people eating a diet of maize and beans.*

First Pilgrim: *Also, as you will recall, we had a lot of starvation and disease, the result being that half of us are dead.*

Second Pilgrim: *Time for a celebration!*

(SCENE FOUR: The Pilgrims and Squanto are seated at a banquet table.)

First Pilgrim: *So here we are, at the (burp) first Thanksgiving.*

Second Pilgrim: *I definitely want the recipe for this alewife dip.*

Fourth Pilgrim: *Hey, Squanto, what are those drums saying?*

Squanto (after listening for a moment): *Lions 14, Bears 7.*

First Pilgrim: *You know, Squanto, without your help, we never would have survived this winter. So we've decided to take over all of North America and pretty much obliterate your culture.*

Squanto: *Sure.*

First Pilgrim: *Really? You don't mind?*

Squanto: *No, not at all.*

First Pilgrim: *Great!*

Squanto: *Try this stuffing.*

HOW TO CURE THE DRUG PROBLEM

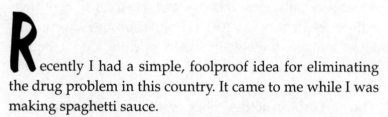

Recently I had a simple, foolproof idea for eliminating the drug problem in this country. It came to me while I was making spaghetti sauce.

I use an ancient Italian spaghetti-sauce recipe that has been handed down through many generations of ancient Italians, as follows:

1. Buy some spaghetti sauce.
2. Heat it up.

Sometimes I add some seasoning to the sauce, to give it a dash of what the Italians call *"joie de vivre"* (literally, "ingredients"). I had purchased, from the supermarket spice section, a small plastic container labeled "Italian Seasoning." My plan was to open this container and sprinkle some seasoning into the sauce.

Already I can hear you veteran consumers out there chortling in good-natured amusement.

"You complete moron," you are chortling. "You actually

thought you could gain access to a product protected by MODERN PACKAGING??"

Yes, I did, and I certainly learned MY lesson. Because it turns out that Italian Seasoning has joined the growing number of products that, For Your Protection, are packaged in containers that you cannot open unless you own a home laser cannon.

This trend started with aspirin. Years ago—ask your grandparents—aspirin was sold in bottles that had removable caps. That system was changed when consumer-safety authorities discovered that certain consumers were taking advantage of this loophole by opening up the bottles and—it only takes a few "bad apples" to spoil things for everybody—ingesting aspirin tablets.

So now aspirin bottles behave very much like stinging insects in nature movies, defending themselves against consumer access via a multilevel security system:

(1) There is a plastic wrapper to keep you from getting at the cap.

(2) The cap, which is patented by the Rubik's Cube company, cannot be removed unless you line an invisible arrow up with an invisible dot while rotating the cap counterclockwise and simultaneously pushing down and pulling up.

(3) In the unlikely event that you get the cap off, the top of the bottle is blocked by a taut piece of extremely feisty foil made from the same impenetrable material used to protect the Space Shuttle during atmospheric reentry.

(4) Underneath the foil is a virtually unremovable wad of cotton the size of a small sheep.

(5) As a final precaution, there is no actual aspirin under-

neath the cotton. There is only a piece of paper listing dangerous side effects, underneath which is . . .

(6) . . . a second piece of paper warning you that the first piece of paper could give you a paper cut.

Even this may not be enough security for the aspirin of tomorrow. At this very moment, packaging scientists are working on an even more secure system, in which the entire aspirin container would be located inside a live sea urchin.

With aspirin leading the way, more and more products are coming out in fiercely protective packaging designed to prevent consumers from consuming them. My Italian Seasoning container featured a foil seal AND a fiendish plastic thing that I could not remove with my bare hands, which meant of course that I had to use my teeth. These days you have to open almost every consumer item by gnawing on the packaging. Go to any typical consumer household and you'll note most of the products—food, medicine, compact discs, appliances, furniture—are covered with bite marks, as though the house is infested with crazed beavers. The floor will be gritty with little chips of consumer teeth. Many consumers are also getting good results by stabbing their products with knives. I would estimate that 58 percent of all serious household accidents result from consumers assaulting packaging designed to improve consumer safety.

Anyway, I finally gnawed my seasoning container open, no doubt activating a tiny transmitter that triggered an alarm in some Spice Security Command Post (WHEEP! WHEEP! WHEEP! INTRUDER GAINING ACCESS TO ITALIAN SEASONING IN SECTOR 19!). While I was stirring my spaghetti sauce, it occurred to me that if we want to eliminate the drug problem in this country, all we have to do is:

1. Make all drugs completely legal and allow them to be sold in supermarkets ("Crack? Aisle 6, next to the Sweet'n Low").
2. Require that the drugs be sold in standard consumer packaging.

My reasoning is that if physically fit, clear-headed consumers can't get into these packages, there's no way that strung-out junkies can. Eventually they'll give up trying to get at their drugs and become useful members of society, or at least attorneys.

I realize that some of you may have questions about this plan. Your most likely concern is: "If dangerous and highly addictive narcotics are sold freely in supermarkets, will the packages be required to have Nutritional Facts labels, like the ones that now helpfully inform consumers of the protein, carbohydrate, vitamin A, vitamin C, calcium, and iron content of products such as Cool Whip Lite?"

Of course they will. Even though, if my plan works as expected, an addict would be unable to consume his heroin purchase, he still has a vital right to know, as an American consumer, that if he DID consume it, he'd be getting only a small percentage of his Daily Requirement of dietary fiber. This is just one of the many benefits we enjoy as residents of this Consumer Paradise. My head aches with pride.

DON'T KNOW MUCH ABOUT HISTORY

Well, you young people have gone and done it again.

I'm talking about the recent study showing that high school students, to quote the Associated Press, "do not know basic facts about American history."

I hate to be a nag, but this is something like the 46,000th consecutive study showing that you young people are not cutting the academic mustard. Do you know how that makes us older people feel? It makes us feel *great*. We go around saying to ourselves: "We may be fat and slow and achy and unhip and have hair sprouting from our noses like June asparagus, but at least we know the basic facts about American history."

According to the Associated Press, "more than half of America's high school seniors do not know the intent of the Monroe Doctrine or the chief goal of United States foreign policy after World War II."

Is that shocking, or what? Of course, to be fair, we have to admit that, for most of the past fifty years, almost *nobody* knew what our foreign policy was. It was a secret. For a while there, in the early 1970s, the only person who knew anything about our foreign policy was Henry Kissinger, who kept it hidden in a secret compartment in his underwear, refusing even to show it to President Nixon, although he did occasionally bring it out to impress actresses he was dating.

In fact, we now know, thanks to recent news reports, that *none* of our postwar presidents really knew what our foreign policy was, because the Central Intelligence Agency (motto: "Proudly Overthrowing Fidel Castro Since 1962") was passing along false information about the Russians. (There is an excellent reason why the CIA did this, but if I told you what it is, I would have to kill you.)

Basically, the CIA led the presidents to believe that the Russians were this well-disciplined, super-advanced military power with all kinds of high-tech atomic laser death rays; whereas in fact the Russians, if they had actually fought us, would have had to rely primarily on the tactic of throwing turnips. So we spent billions of dollars on items such as the Stealth bomber, which by the way we are still building, in case we ever need to sneak an airplane over there to drop bombs on, say, a Burger King.

But my point is that most of us had no idea what the U.S. foreign policy was until the election of Bill Clinton, who, to his credit, has established a clear and consistent foreign policy, which is as follows: Whenever the president of the United States gets anywhere near any foreign head of state, living or dead, he gives that leader a big old hug. This has proven to be an effective way to get foreign leaders to do what we want: Many heads of state are willing to sign any random document that President Clinton thrusts in front of them, without reading it, just so he will stop embracing them. This is how the prime minister of Sweden, in a recent visit to the White House, wound up purchasing nearly $4,000 worth of Amway products.

But getting back to the issue at hand, which is the intent of the Monroe Doctrine: I am shocked that more than half of today's high-school seniors do not know what it is. This kind of ignorance was NOT tolerated when I was a student at Pleasantville (New York) High School, where I studied history under a teacher named—I am not making this up—Oscar Fossum. No sir, we *learned* our history back then, and we learned it the hard way: By being subjected to surprise quizzes in which we had to write 200-word essay-style answers to questions on topics we knew virtually nothing about, such as:

The Intent of the Monroe Doctrine

"The Monroe Doctrine is, without a doubt, one of the most important and famous historical doctrines ever to be set forth in doctrine form. And yet, by the same token, we must ask ourselves: Why? What is the quality that sets this particular doctrine—the Monroe Doctrine—apart from all the others? There can be no question that the answer to this question is: the intent. For when we truly understand the intent of a doctrine such as the Monroe Doctrine, or for that matter any other doctrine, only then can we truly know exactly what that doctrine was intended to accomplish as far as doctrinal intention is concerned. This has been an issue of great significance to historians and human beings alike throughout the distinguished history of this great country that we call, simply, 'the United States of America,' a country that has produced more than its share of famous doctrines and great heroes and, yes, educators of the caliber of Mr. Fossum, doing such a superb job of preparing the young people of tomorrow for the day when we, as a society and yet by the same token also as a nation, finally reach 200 words."

See what I mean, young people? Thanks to my solid academic training, today I can write hundreds of words on virtually any topic without possessing a shred of information, which is how I got a good job in journalism. So I urge you to work hard in school and learn your history, because—who knows?—one of you could be the next Abraham Lincoln, inventor of the steam engine.

THIS POET DON'T KNOW IT

Recently I got a very nice computer-generated letter from an outfit called the National Library of Poetry.

"Dear Dave," the letter begins. "Over the past year or so we have been reviewing the thousands of poems submitted to us, as well as examining the poetic accomplishments of people whose poetry has been featured in various anthologies released by other poetry publishers. After an exhaustive examination of this poetic artistry, The National Library of Poetry has decided to publish a collection of new poems written by THE BEST POETS we have encountered.

"I am pleased to tell you, Dave, that you have been selected to appear in this special edition: *Best Poems of 1995* . . . The poem which you will submit for this edition has been accepted for publication sight unseen on the basis of your previous poetic accomplishments."

You talk about feeling honored. It's not every day that a person who does not, technically, write poetry is selected as one of the top poets for a year that has not, technically, occurred yet.

Oh, I know what some of you are thinking. You're thinking, "Dave, you wienerhead, they don't really think you're a leading poet. They got your name from some mailing list, and they'll publish any drivel you send in, because what they REALLY want to do is throw a book together and then sell it to a bunch of pathetic loser wannabe 'poets' for some absurdly inflated price like $50."

Well that just shows how much YOU know. Because it turns out that *Best Poems of 1995* is now available at a special pre-publication discount price of just $49.95. But listen to what you get: You get "a superb collection of over 3,000 poems on every topic," as well as "an heirloom quality publication" with "imported French marbleized covers."

I called the number listed on the National Library of Poetry letterhead; a pleasant-sounding woman answered, and I asked her which specific poetic accomplishments of mine the judges had reviewed before selecting me as one of the Best Poets.

"Um," she said, "we don't have that available right now. All that information is closed in a backup file system."

I frankly have had very few poetic accomplishments. I once thought about writing poems for a line of thoughtful greeting cards, but I finished only one, which went:

Thinking of you
At this special time
And hoping your organ
Removal went fine.

Of course I have to produce an entirely new poem for *Best Poems of 1995*. I asked the woman at the National Library of Poetry if there were any special literary criteria involved; she said the only one was that the poem had to be, quote, "Twenty lines or less."

I was happy to hear that. If there's one thing I hate, it's a long poem. And if there's another thing I hate, it's a poem wherein the poet refuses to tell you what the hell he's talking about. For example, when I was an English major in college, we spent *weeks* trying to get a handle on an extremely dense poem called *The Waste Land* by T.S. Eliot, only to conclude, after endless droning hours of classroom discussion, that the poem was expressing angst about the modern era. I felt like calling Eliot up and saying, "Listen, T.S., the next time you want to express angst, just EXPRESS it, okay? Just say 'Yo! I'm feeling some angst over here!' "

I believe that if some of your former big-name poets such as Homer and Milton (neither of whom, to my knowledge, was invited to be in *Best Poems of 1995*) had observed the National Library of Poetry's twenty-line limit, their careers would be in a lot better shape today.

Anyway, I wrote a poem for *Best Poems of 1995*. I call it, simply, "Love." Here it is:

> *O love is a feeling that makes a person strive*
> *To crank out one of the Best Poems of 1995;*
> *Love is what made Lassie the farm dog run back to the farmhouse to alert*
> *   little Timmy's farm family whenever little Timmy fell into a dangerous*
> *   farm pit;*
> *Love is a feeling that will not go away, like a fungus in your armpit;*
> *So the bottom line is that there will always be lovers*

Wishing to express their love in an heirloom quality book with imported
  French marbleized covers;
Which at $49.95 a pop multiplied by 3,000 poets
Works out to gross literary revenues of roughly $150,000, so it's
A good bet that whoever thought up the idea of publishing this book
Doesn't care whether this last line rhymes.

I sent this poem in to the folks at the National Library of Poetry. If you think that you, too, have what it takes to be one of the Best Poets of 1995, you might want to send them a poem of your own; their address is Box 704, Owings Mills, MD 21117. Tell them Dave sent you.

And T.S., if you send something in, for God's sake keep it simple.

THE MEDICAL BOOM

I will frankly admit that I am afraid of medical care. I trace this fear to my childhood, when as far as I could tell, the medical profession's reaction to every physical problem I developed, including nearsightedness, was to give me a tetanus shot. Not only that, but the medical professionals would always lie about it.

"You'll hardly feel it!" they'd say, coming at me with a needle the size of a harpoon.

As a child, I was more afraid of tetanus shots than, for example, Dracula. Granted, Dracula would come into your room at night and bite into your neck and suck out all your blood, but there was a positive side to this; namely, you could turn into a bat and stay out all night. Whereas I could see no pluses with the tetanus shot.

Of course today I no longer have this childish phobia, because, as a mature adult, I can lie.

"I just had a tetanus shot this morning!" I can say, if the issue ever arises. "Eight of them, in fact!"

But I'm still afraid of medical care. And I'm not encouraged by TV medical dramas such as *ER*. If you watch these shows, you've probably noticed that whenever some pathetic civilian gets wheeled into the hospital emergency room on a stretcher, he or she is immediately pounced upon by enough medical personnel to form a hospital softball league, all competing to see who can do the scariest thing to the victim. Apparently there's a clause in the standard Television Performers' Contract stating that every character in a medical drama gets to take a crack at emergency patients:

> **First Doctor:** *I'll give him a shot!*
> **Second Doctor:** *I'll pound his chest!*
> **Third Doctor:** *I'll stick a tube way up his nose!*
> **Fourth Doctor:** *I'll find an unoccupied section of his body and cut it open for no good reason!*
> **Janitor:** *I'll wash his mouth out with a toilet brush!*

Now you're probably saying: "Dave, you big baby, those are just *TV shows*. In real life, bad things do not happen to people who fall into the hands of medical care."

Excuse me for one second while I laugh so hard that my keyboard is short-circuited by drool. Because I happen to be holding in my hand a bulletin-board notice that was sent to me by a Vermont orthopedic surgeon named either "David H. Bahnson, M.D.," or "Oee Bali," depending on whether you're reading his letterhead or his signature.

Dr. Bahnson told me, in a phone interview, that he found this notice over the "scrub sink," which is the place where doctors wash their hands after they operate so that they won't get flecks of your vital organs on their Lexus upholstery.

No, seriously, the scrub sink is where they wash their hands *before* operating, and Dr. Bahnson said that this notice had been prominently displayed there for several months. It is titled—I am not making this up—"EMERGENCY PROCEDURE: FIGHTING FIRE ON THE SURGICAL PATIENT."

Yes, you read that correctly. Dr. Bahnson told me that, although it has not happened to him, fires sometimes break out on patients during surgery, particularly when hot medical implements accidentally come into contact with surgical drapes.

The bulletin-board notice discusses two types of situations: "small fire on the patient" and "large fire on the patient." There are step-by-step instructions for dealing with both of these; Step 3 under "large fire on the patient," for example is: "Care for the patient."

I was surprised that the procedure was so definite. You'd think that, what with all these medical lawsuits, the instructions would call for more caution on the part of the doctors. ("Mrs. Dweemer, we think you might be on fire, but we won't know for sure until we have a specialist fly in from Switzerland to take a look.")

Now before I get a lot of irate mail from the medical community, let me stress that not all surgical patients catch on fire. Some of them also explode. I am referring here to a November article from *The Medical Post*, sent in by alert reader Lauren Leighton, headlined: "BEWARE EXPLODING PATIENTS." This article states that nitrous oxide—which is sometimes used as an anesthetic in stomach surgery—can get mixed up with intestinal gases, which have been proven to be highly combustible in countless scientific experiments conducted in fraternity houses. If this mixture is ignited by a spark from a surgical implement such as an electric cautery, the result can be what the article refers to as "intra-abdominal fires."

In what could be the single most remarkable statement that I have ever read in a medical article, one expert is quoted as saying—I swear this is a real quote—"Patients aren't exploding all over, but there is potential for it."

Ha ha! I certainly am feeling reassured!

No, really, I'm sure we're talking about a very small number of patients exploding or catching on fire. So if you, personally, are scheduled to undergo surgery, you needn't give this matter another thought, assuming that you have taken the basic precaution of having a personal sprinkler system installed on your body.

No, seriously, I'm sure your operation will go just fine. And even in the unlikely event that you do explode, you may rest assured that, no matter how many pieces you wind up in, every one of those pieces will, in accordance with modern medical standards, receive a tetanus shot.

GOBBLE, GOBBLE, EEEEEEEEEK!

We are approaching the Thanksgiving holiday, when we pause to reflect on our blessings by eating pretty much non-stop for an entire day, then staggering off to bed, still chewing, with wads of stuffing clinging to our hair.

It's a spiritual time, yes, but it can also be a tragic time if an inadequately cooked turkey gives us salmonella poisoning, which occurs when tiny turkey-dwelling salmon get into our blood, swim upstream, and spawn in our brains (this is probably what happened to Ross Perot). That's why the American Turkey and Giblet Council recommends that, to insure proper preparation, you cook your turkey in a heated oven for at least two full quarters of the Vikings-Lions game, then give a piece to your dog and observe it closely for symptoms such as vomiting, running for president, etc.

Someday, perhaps, we won't have to take these precautions, not if the U.S. government approves a radical new concept in poultry safety being proposed by a company in Rancho Cucamonga, California. I am not making up Rancho Cucamonga: It's a real place whose odd-sounding name, if you look it up in your Spanish-English dictionary, turns out to mean "Cucamonga Ranch." I am also not making up the poultry-safety advance, which was discussed in a lengthy news story by Randyl Drummer in the May 16 issue of the *Inland Valley Daily Bulletin*, sent in by many alert readers. Before I quote from this story, I need to issue a:

WARNING TO TASTEFUL READERS: You should NOT—I repeat, NOT—read the rest of this column if you are likely to be in any way offended by the term "turkey rectums."

The story appears on the *Daily Bulletin's* business page, under the headline PACER BACKING NEW USE FOR GLUE. It begins, I swear, as follows:

"RANCHO CUCAMONGA—Jim Munn hopes that the government and the poultry industry will get behind his process for gluing chicken and turkey rectums."

Jim Munn, the story explains, is the president of a company called Pacer Technology, which makes Super Glue. Munn, the story states, believes that meat contamination can be reduced by "gluing shut the rectal cavities of turkeys and chicken broilers." (Needless to say, this would be done *after* the chickens and turkeys have gone to that Big Barnyard in the Sky; otherwise, everybody involved would have to be paid a ridiculous amount of money.)

The story states that "Munn became intrigued by a poultry rectal glue product after a federal inspector contacted him and said he had used Super Glue on a turkey."

I frankly find it hard to believe that a federal employee would admit such a thing, after what happened to Bob Packwood, but Jim Munn thought it was a terrific concept.

He plans to market the product under the name—get ready—"Rectite."

"Poultry officials applaud the idea," states the story.

I do, too. I am all for gluing turkeys shut; in fact, I think they should be glued shut *permanently*, because, as a consumer, I do not wish to come into contact with those gross organs, necks, glands, etc. that come packed inside them. There are few scarier experiences in life than having to put your unarmed hand inside the cold, clammy recesses of a darkened turkey and pull those things out, never knowing when one of them will suddenly come to life like the creature in the movie *Alien*, leap off your kitchen counter, and skitter around snacking on household residents.

So I urge you to telephone your congressperson immediately and state your position on this issue clearly and forcefully, as follows: "I favor gluing turkey rectums!" And while you have your congressperson on the line, you might want to point out that the Walt Disney Company is secretly using cartoon movies to promote sex. Yes. I have here a document from an organization called the American Life League, titled "OFFICIAL STATEMENT ON DISNEY'S PERVERTED ANIMATION." The document states that Disney has been putting smut into its cartoon movies, and cites the following examples, which I am still not making up:

- In Aladdin, *"when Prince Ababwa calls on Princess Jasmine on her balcony, a voice whispers, 'Good teenagers, take off your clothes.'"* The document further asserts that in the same movie, Abu the monkey says a bad word.
- In The Little Mermaid, *the officiator in the wedding scene "is obviously sexually aroused." Not only that, but*

"the box cover of The Little Mermaid *contains a phallic symbol in the center of the royal castle."*

- *In* The Lion King, *when Simba plops down, "The cloud of dust that he stirs up, to the upper left of his head, forms the letters S-E-X." (Which, if you remove the hyphens, spells "sex.")*

None of this surprises me. I have been suspicious of the Disney people ever since it was first pointed out to me, years ago, that Donald Duck does not wear pants. There is WAY more of this perversion going on than we are aware of, and it is not limited to Disney. Look at the shape of the Life Savers package! Are we supposed to believe that's *coincidence*?

No, this kind of thing is everywhere, and today I am calling on you readers, as concerned individuals with a lot of spare time, to look for instances of hidden perversion in commercial products, then report them to me by sending a postcard to: Smut Patrol, c/o Dave Barry, *Miami Herald*, Miami, FL 33132.

Working together, we WILL get to the bottom of this. And then we will glue it shut.

MESSAGE FROM THE STARS

We are not alone.

I make this statement in light of an article sent to me by alert reader Steve Kennedy, who found it in an academic journal called *Popular Music and Society*. The article, written by a college professor named Cherrill P. Heaton, is titled "Air Ball: Spontaneous Large Group Precision Chanting."

The article concerns a phenomenon that often occurs at basketball games when a visiting player shoots an "air ball"—a shot that misses everything. Immediately, the crowd, in a sportsmanlike effort to cause this player to commit suicide, will start chanting "AIR-ball . . . AIR-ball . . ."

Professor Heaton, who teaches English but is also interested in music, noticed an odd thing about the "Air Ball" chant: The crowd members always seemed to start at precisely the same time, and in perfect tune with each other.

"As any director of a church choir or secular chorus knows," Professor Heaton writes, "getting a mere twenty or thirty trained singers to sing or chant together and in tune is not always easy. Yet without direction . . . thousands of strangers massed in indoor auditoriums and arenas are able, if stimulated by an air ball, to chant 'Air Ball' in tonal and rhythmic unison."

But there's more. Using his VCR, Professor Heaton taped a bunch of basketball games; he discovered that, no matter where the games were played, almost all the crowds chanted "Air Ball" in *the same key*—namely, F, with the "Air" being sung on an F note, and the "Ball" on a D note.

This is an amazing musical achievement for Americans, who are not noted for their skill at singing in unison. Listen to a random group of Americans attempting to sing "Happy Birthday," and you will note that at any given moment they somehow manage to emit more different notes, total, than there are group members, creating a somber, droning sound such as might be created by severely asthmatic bagpipers, so that the birthday person, rather than feeling happy, winds up weeping into the cake. It's even worse when Americans at sporting events attempt to sing "The Star-Spangled Banner," because not only does this song contain an estimated 54,000 notes, but also the crowd has only the vaguest notion of what the words are, so what you hear is a vaguely cattle-like sound created by thousands of people murmuring uncertainly, in every conceivable key, about the ramparts red gleaming. And yet according to Professor Heaton, somehow these same sports fans, all over the country, almost always spontaneously chant "Air Ball" in the same key, F.

I decided to check Professor Heaton's findings myself. Under the carefully controlled scientific conditions of my living room, I chanted "Air Ball" out loud several times. I then picked up my electric guitar, which I keep close to my computer for those occasions when, in the course of my research, I develop an urgent journalistic need to sing "Mony Mony." Using this guitar, I figured out which key I had chanted "Air Ball" in: It was F.

Still skeptical, I called my office at the *Miami Herald*. The phone was answered in a spontaneous manner by a writer named Meg Laughlin.

I said: "Meg, I want you to do the chant that basketball fans do when a visiting player shoots an air ball."

And Meg, with no further prompting, said: "Nanny nanny boo boo?"

Meg is not a big basketball fan.

Continuing my research, I called Charlie Vincent, a professional sports columnist for the *Detroit Free Press*, who claims he has never sung on key in his life, and who immediately, without prompting, chanted "Air Ball" smack dab in F. Then I called professional musician and basketball fan Al Kooper; he not only chanted "Air Ball" in F, but also told me that, back in the 1960s, he used to spend hours eavesdropping on people and painstakingly writing down the musical notes that they used in ordinary conversation.

"Hey, cool!" I said. "What did you do with this information?"

"I lost it," he said.

Finally I decided to try the acid test: I called my current and former editors, Tom Shroder and Gene Weingarten, who are the two least musically talented human beings on the face of the Earth. These guys could not make a teakettle whistle; it would indicate that it was ready by holding up a little sign that said "tweet."

Because Tom and Gene are severely rhythmically impaired, neither one could actually *chant* "Air Ball"; they both just nervously blurted it out a few times very fast—*airballairballairball*—and there was no way to determine, without sensitive instruments, what, if any, musical key they were in. But it *could* have been F.

Anyway, my research convinced me that Professor Heaton is correct: Something is causing Americans to chant "Air Ball" in F. But what? I believe that the most logical explanation—you probably thought of this—is: extraterrestrials. As you know if you watch the TV documentary series *The X-Files*, when anything weird happens, extraterrestrials are almost always responsible. In this case, beings from another galaxy are probably trying to communicate with us by transmitting powerful radio beams that penetrate basketball fans' brains and cause them to "spontaneously" chant in the key of F. I imagine that eventually the aliens will switch the fans to another key, such as A, and then maybe C, and so on until the aliens have musically spelled out some intergalactic message to humanity, such as "FACE A DEAD CABBAGE."

Or it could be something else. I have no idea what they're trying to tell us; I just know we'd better do what they say. And now if you'll excuse me, I'm feeling an overpowering urge to do "the wave."

READY TO WEAR

Today's Topic Is: Fashion Tips for Men

This topic was suggested by a letter from John Cog of Norfolk, Virginia. Here's the entire text:

"How come when I'm standing in front of a full-length mirror with nothing on but socks, white socks look OK, but dark-colored socks make me look cheap and sleazy?"

This letter was passed along to me by my Research Department, Judi Smith, who attached a yellow stick-on note that says: "This is true." Judi did not say how she happens to *know* it's true; apparently—and I'm sure there's a perfectly innocent explanation—she has seen John Cog of Norfolk, Virginia, wearing nothing but socks.

But the point is that dark socks, as a lone fashion accessory, create a poor impression. This is a known fact that has been verified in scientific experiments wherein fashion researchers put little white socks on one set of naked laboratory rats, and dark socks on another, then exposed both groups to a panel of leading business executives such as Bill

Gates, who indicated that they would be "somewhat more likely" to hire from the white-sock group, should their personnel needs ever include a rat.

What this means, men, is that if you're dressing for an important job interview, church supper, meeting with my Research Department, or other occasion where you could wind up wearing nothing but socks, they should be white.

Likewise, if you're going to be wearing just your underwear, you should always tuck your undershirt way down into your underpants. This is the "look" favored by the confident, sharp-dressing men found in the underwear section of the now-defunct Sears catalog, who are often depicted standing around in Rotary-Club-like groups, looking relaxed and smiling, as if to say: "Our undershirts are tucked way down into our underpants, and we could not feel better about it!"

These men live in Sears Catalog Men's Underwear Town, where all the residents, including on-duty police officers, wear only underwear. All the residents are always in a good mood because they live only a few pages away from Sears Catalog Women's Underwear Town, which is occupied by hundreds of women who stand around all day wearing nothing but brassieres and underpants and thinking nothing of it. Sometimes, late at night, they all get together for wild parties in the Power Tools section.

The happy mood in the Sears underwear towns stands in stark contrast to the mood in Calvin Klein Perfume-Ad Town, where you'd *think* people would be ecstatic, because they're always writhing around in naked coeducational groups like worms in a bait bucket, but they always have troubled expressions on their faces, as if they're thinking:

"*Somebody* in this coeducational group had Mexican food for lunch."

One last underwear tip: No doubt your mom always told you that your underwear should be clean and free of holes or stains, because you might get in a car crash and be taken, unconscious, to the hospital, and people would see your underwear and possibly ridicule it. Your mom was absolutely right, as we can see from the following unretouched transcript from the emergency room of a major hospital:

> **Doctor:** *What do we have here?*
> **Nurse:** *We have a car-crash victim who has severe head trauma and a broken neck and massive internal injuries and is spewing blood like a fire hydrant.*
> **Doctor (briskly):** *Okay, let's take a look at his underwear . . . WHOA! How do you get Cheez Whiz THERE?*
> **(Laughter from everybody in the emergency room, including gunshot victims.)**

Our final fashion tip for men concerns those special occasions when, for whatever reason, you want to wear something on top of your underwear. What style of clothing is right for you? The answer—taking into consideration your particular age, build, coloring, and personality—is: "clothing that has been picked out by a woman." Because the sad truth is that males, as a group, have the fashion sense of cement.

Oh, I realize that there are exceptions—men who know how to pick out elegant suits and perfectly color-coordinated accessories. But for every man walking around looking tasteful, there are at least ten men walking around wearing orange plaid Bermuda shorts with non-matching boxer shorts sticking out above AND below, and sometimes also poking out through the fly.

Men are genetically programmed to select ugly clothing. This dates back millions of years, to when primitive tribal men, responsible for defending their territory, would deck themselves out in face paint, animal heads, and nose bones so as to look really hideous and scare off enemy tribes. If some prehistoric tribal warriors had somehow got hold of modern golf clothing, they would have ruled the rain forest.

In conclusion, men, please remember that the fashion tips contained in this column are just the "basics." To learn more about the current men's fashion "scene," get a copy of *Esquire* or *GQ* and study the ads and articles presenting the latest styles, making a mental note to never, ever wear any of them, because unless you're a male model, you'd look stupid. Just wear a regular blue suit like everybody else and try to have both shoes the same color. You can get that Cheez Whiz out with bleach.

FORE PLAY

I t's a gloriously sunny day in Miami, and I'm standing in a semicircle of maybe 500 people on a carpet of lush, sweet-smelling, green-glinting grass, the kind that makes you want to get naked and roll around on your back like a dog.

But the people around me are not doing that. They're silent and solemn, like a church congregation, except that a lot of them are smoking cigars. They're staring intently at some tiny figures way off in the distance. I'm staring, too, but I can't quite make out what the figures are doing.

Suddenly the crowd murmurs, and 500 heads jerk skyward in unison. I still can't see anything. The crowd holds its breath, waiting, waiting, and then suddenly . . .

PLOP

. . . a little white ball falls from the sky, lands in the middle of the semicircle, and starts rolling. Immediately the crowd members are shouting at it angrily.

"Bite!" they shout, spewing saliva and cigar flecks. "BITE!!" This is how they tell the ball they want it to stop rolling.

The ball, apparently fearing for its life, stops. The crowd members applaud and cheer wildly. They're acting as though the arrival of this ball is the highlight of their lives.

Which maybe it is. These are, after all, golf fans. And this ball was personally hit by—prepare to experience a heart seizure—*Jack Nicklaus.*

This exciting moment in sports occurred at the Doral-Ryder Open golf tournament, an event on the professional golf tour, wherein the top golfers from all over the world gather together to see who can take the longest amount of time to actually hit the ball.

I don't know about you, but when I play golf—which I have done a total of three times in my life—I don't waste a lot of time. I just grab a club, stride briskly to the ball, take a hearty swing, then check to see if the ball has moved from its original location. If it hasn't, I take another hearty swing, repeating this process as necessary until the ball is gone, which is my cue to get out another ball, because I know from harsh experience that I will never in a million years find the first one. I keep this up until there are no balls left, which is my cue to locate the part of the golfing facility where they sell beer. In other words, I play an exciting, nonstop-action brand of golf that would be ideal for spectators, except for the fact that most of them would be killed within minutes.

Your professional golfer, on the other hand, does not even *think* about hitting a ball until he has conducted a complete geological and meteorological survey of the situation—circling the ball warily, as though it were a terrorist device, checking it out from every possible angle; squatting and squinting; checking the wind; taking soil samples; analyzing satellite photographs; testing the area for traces of O.J. Simpson's DNA, etc. Your professional golfer takes longer to line up a six-foot putt than the Toyota corporation takes to turn raw iron ore into a Corolla.

I know that it may sound boring to watch grown men

squat for minutes on end, but when you see a pro tournament in person—when you're actually watching these world-class golfers line up their shots—it is in fact *unbelievably* boring. At least it was for me. I would rank it, as a spectator sport, with transmission repair.

"HIT THE BALL, ALREADY!" is what I wanted to shout at Jack Nicklaus, but I did not, because the crowd would have turned on me, and my lifeless body would have been found later buried in a sand trap, covered with cigar burns. Because these fans worship the golfers, and they seem to be truly fascinated by the squatting and squinting process. The more time that passed with virtually nothing happening, the more excited the golf fans became, until finally, when Jack got ready to take the extreme step of actually hitting the ball, everybody was nearly crazy with anticipation, although nobody was making a peep, because putting is an extremely difficult and highly technical activity that—unlike, for example, brain surgery—must be performed in absolute silence.

And so, amid an atmosphere of tension comparable to that of a Space Shuttle launch, Jack finally bent over the ball, drew back his putter, and gently tapped the ball.

"GET IN THE HOLE!" the crowd screamed at the ball. "GET IN THE HOLE!"

The ball, of course, did not go in the hole. Your world-class golfers miss a surprising number of short putts. Too much squatting, if you ask me.

"NO!" shouted the crowd, when the ball stopped, maybe an inch from the hole. Some men seemed to be near tears; some were cursing openly. These people were *furious* at the ball. They did not blame Jack. Jack worked *hard* to line up this putt, and here this idiot ball *let him down*.

But Jack was magnanimous. He tapped the ball in, and the fans applauded wildly, as well they should have, because it is not every day that you see a person cause a little ball to roll six feet.

When Jack had acknowledged the applause, the next famous world-class golfer in his group, John Daly, began considering the many, many complex factors involved in his putt, which he will probably be ready to attempt no later than June. Let me know if he makes it. I'll be in the grass just beyond the refreshment area, rolling around like a dog.

This is me getting ready to go for a ride in a stunt biplane. It was tremendously exciting and fun. Then we took off, and it was horrible. This happened in 1987, and I am still nauseated.

WARP SPEED

H ere's what I want you to do: Open your mouth wide. Now take your index finger and stick it WAAAYYYY down your throat and hold it there until your digestive system is in Violent Reverse Thrust Mode.

Congratulations! You've just experienced what it feels like to fly in a fighter jet. I know this because I recently went up in a high-performance Air Force F-16 fighter equipped with an extremely powerful engine, sophisticated electronics, spectacular aerobatic capabilities, and—thank God—a barf bag.

There was no beverage-cart service.

The way I got into this was, I spoke at a banquet for personnel at the Homestead (Florida) Air Reserve Base, which is slowly recovering after having had large sectors of it blown into another dimension by Hurricane Andrew. A banquet organizer had suggested that I might want to go up in an F-16, and some friendly fighter pilots from the 93rd Fighter Squadron convinced me (there WAS beverage service at this banquet) that this would be a lot of fun.

Valuable Tip: Never assume that you and fighter pilots

have the same definition of "fun." Your fighter pilot is not a normal individual. Your fighter pilot is an individual who, as a child, liked to ride his bicycle "no-hands." You may also have done this, but your future fighter pilot was doing it on the roof of his house. The fact that these pilots have grown up and received a lot of training and been entrusted by the government with multimillion-dollar aircraft does not change the fact that they are also—and I say this with respect—completely out of their minds.

But I was feeling brave when I arrived at Homestead Air Reserve Base, ready for my preflight training. Friendly Air Force personnel got me a flight suit; while I was putting it on in the locker room, I noticed that there was a little gold plaque over each urinal, each saying something like "MAJ. GEN. (Name) RELIEVED HIMSELF HERE SEPTEMBER 9, 1989." Then I noticed similar gold plaques over the sinks. Then I saw a plaque on the washing machine, reading: "THE ENTIRE 906TH TACTICAL FIGHTER GROUP RE-LIEVED THEMSELVES HERE MARCH 8, 1991."

Fighter-pilot humor. And I was *trusting* these guys.

Next I underwent an hour of Egress Training, which is when you learn how you get out of the airplane if something goes wrong ("although probably nothing will," they keep telling you). How you get out is: very, very fast. In fact, your seat is actually a small but powerful rocket that will blast you 900 feet straight up if you yank on the yellow handle between your legs, but you're supposed to do this only if the pilot yells "BAIL OUT BAIL OUT BAIL OUT"—he has to say it three times—and you definitely want to have your head back when you yank it unless you want your kneecaps to pass completely through your eye sockets, which would be bad because you need to check to make sure your parachute has deployed, because if it hasn't you should yank on this other yellow lever over here, and if you're coming down over water you need to inflate your life preserver by pulling on these two red knobs, but first you have to get rid of your oxygen mask by pressing outward on these two metal tabs and yanking the mask forward and . . .

. . . and so on for an hour. Correctly egressing a fighter jet requires WAY more knowledge than medical school.

After Egress Training, the pilot, Major Derek Rydholm, gave me a Preflight Briefing in which he demonstrated, using a blackboard eraser, some of the aerial maneuvers we'd be doing.

"We'll be simulating at attack situation like this," he'd say, moving the eraser around in rapid little arcs. "We'll be feeling some g-forces."

I now realize that, right after we left the briefing room, the eraser threw up.

Actually, my F-16 ride went pretty well at first. Sitting behind Derek in the two-person cockpit, I felt nervous, but my physical discomfort was fairly minor.

Then we took off.

We took off with afterburners. It was like in *Star Trek*, when they go to Warp Speed. Then we made an unbelievably sudden, violent right turn that made me feel like a clove in a giant garlic press and separated my stomach from the rest of my body by at least two football fields.

And that was just *taking off*. After that we did attack maneuvers. We did rolls. We broke the sound barrier and then flew straight up for three miles. Then we flew upside down. My stomach never caught up with us. It's still airborne over the Florida Keys, awaiting landing instructions. Here's the conversation Derek and I had over the intercom:

Derek: That's called an aileron roll.
Me: BLEAAARRGGGHH
Derek: You okay back there?
Me: HOOOGGGGHHHH

I'm not saying it wasn't thrilling. It was. I am deeply indebted to Derek Rydholm and the 93rd Fighter Squadron and the entire U.S. Air Force for enabling me to be among the very few people who can boast that they have successfully lost their lunch upside down at five times the Earth's gravitational pull. And despite my discomfort, and the reservations I've expressed in this column, I can honestly say that, if I ever get a chance to go up again, I'll let you go instead. Although you probably won't get to ride in the plane I used. I think they had to burn it.

DASHING THROUGH THE SNOW...

Skiing is an exciting winter sport, but it is not for everybody. For example, it is not for sane people. Sane people look at skiing, and they say: "WAIT a minute. I'm supposed to attach slippery objects to my feet and get on a frozen chair dangling from a scary-looking wire; then get dumped off on a snow-covered slope so steep that the mountain goats are wearing seat belts; and then, if by some miracle I am able to get back down without killing myself, I'm supposed to do this AGAIN??"

As I get older—which I am currently doing at the rate of about five years per year—this is more and more how I view skiing. I've been looking for an alternative winter sport that does not force a person to become so intimately involved with gravity. And so recently I went to Idaho (official state motto: "Convenient to Montana") to experience two winter sports that seemed better-suited to the mature sportsperson in the sense that you can do them while sitting down. In an effort to make my trip as tax-deductible as humanly possible, I've decided to write a two-part series about these sports. This week's Featured Winter Sport is: snowmobiling.

A snowmobile is a high-performance motorized vehicle mounted on a track and skis that enable it to travel rapidly deep into remote snow-covered wilderness areas, where it gets stuck. Of course I didn't know this when I rented one. I knew nothing, which is why I also rented snowmobiles for my fifteen-year-old son, Rob, and his fourteen-year-old friend Ryan. It was going to be a fun thing for us three guys to do together; that is what I was saying to myself as I signed the legal release form (". . . the undersigned further agrees that he has not actually read this form and just wants to get on the snowmobile already and would in fact cheerfully sign anything placed in front of him including a document granting us the right to keep both his ears as souvenirs").

We rented our snowmobiles at a place called the Smiley Creek Lodge, which is in a place called Smiley Creek, which pretty much consists of the Smiley Creek Lodge. We also rented helmets and jumpsuits so that we would look as much as possible like the Invasion of the Dork Tourists from Space. A very nice man showed us how to make the snowmobiles go. He seemed extremely calm, considering that he was turning three powerful and expensive machines over to two adolescent boys and a humor columnist. I thought he'd give us detailed instructions regarding where we should go, but basically all he said was that we should make an effort to remain in Idaho.

This did not prove to be so easy; not with Rob and Ryan at the controls. They are wonderful and intelligent boys, but they have the common sense of table salt. It's not their fault: Their brains have not yet developed the Fear Lobe. If you give them control over a motorized vehicle, they are going to go at the fastest possible speed, which on a modern snowmobile turns out to be 14,000 miles per hour. They were leaving trails of flaming snow behind them. I tried to exercise Adult Supervision by yelling "HEY! GUYS! BE CAREFUL! HEY!" but they couldn't hear me, because sound travels only so fast.

So off we went, into the snow-covered wilds of Idaho, with the two Flaming No-Judgment Blurs roaring ahead, followed at an increasing distance by the Rapidly Aging Shouting Man. We would have been inside the Arctic Circle by nightfall if Ryan had not driven into the creek. It was not his fault. He didn't see the creek. Some idiot had failed to put up the freeway-style sign with fifteen-foot-high letters saying "CREEK," and so Ryan naturally drove in to it.

Since your model snowmobile weighs as much as a freight locomotive, we were unable to pull Ryan's out, so he got on the back of mine and we all rode sheepishly back to the Smiley Creek Lodge. There we learned that another tourist party was also having problems: A man had gotten himself and his son stuck in deep snow, and they couldn't get out. The man's wife, who had not been wild about the snowmobiling idea in the first place, was informing the lodge personnel that she wanted her son back, but as far as she was concerned, they could leave her husband out there. (She was kidding.) (Sort of.)

While this drama was unfolding, *another* group of tourists returned and announced that they, too, had planted a snowmobile somewhere out in Idaho.

None of this bothered the nice snowmobile-renting man. He calmly called in some local Idaho men—soft-spoken, strong, competent-looking men, the kind of men who never get their snowmobiles stuck and could probably survive for weeks in the wilderness by eating pinecones. They went out and rescued the father and son, and then they went and pulled out all of the stuck snowmobiles. I realized that this was routine for them; on any given winter day, probably two-thirds of the Idaho population is busy pulling tourist-abandoned snowmobiles out of creeks, snowbanks, trees, mine shafts, condominiums, etc.

So it all ended well, and the boys thought snowmobiling was the coolest thing we could have done short of blowing up a building. I, on the other hand, was looking for a more restful mode of snow transportation, and I'm pleased to report that I found one: It requires no gasoline, it goes at a nice safe speed, and it doesn't get stuck. On the other hand, it emits an amazing amount of weewee.

NEXT WEEK: Dogsledding.

MUSH!

This is the second part of a two-part series titled "Recreational Winter Sports That You Can Do Sitting Down." Last week, in part one, I discussed snowmobiling, with my key finding being that you should not go snowmobiling with adolescent boys unless your recreational goal is total cardiac arrest. Today I'll discuss a sport that is more relaxing as well as far more fragrant: Dogsled-riding.

A dogsled is—follow me carefully here—a sled that is pulled by dogs. And if you think that dogs are not strong enough to pull a sled, then you have never been walking a dog on a leash when a squirrel ran past. Even a small dog in this situation will generate one of the most powerful forces known to modern science. In some squirrel-infested areas, it is not at all unusual to see a frantically barking dog racing down the street, wearing a leash that is attached to a bouncing, detached arm.

Historians believe that the dogsled was invented thousands of years ago when an Alaskan Eskimo attached a pair of crude runners to a frame, hitched this contrivance to a pack of dogs, climbed aboard, and wound up in Brazil. This taught the remaining Eskimos that if they were going to build another one of these things, it should definitely have brakes. Today, dogsleds are mainly used in races, the most famous one being the Alaskan Iditarod, in which competitors race from Anchorage to Nome, with the winner getting a cash prize of $50,000, which just about covers the winner's Chap Stick expenses.

I took a far more modest dogsled ride, up and down a smallish mountain near Hailey, Idaho, on a sled operated by Sun Valley Sled Dog Adventures. This is a small company started by a very nice young guy named Brian Camilli, who plans to win the Iditarod someday, and who bought his first sled dogs five years ago with what was going to be his college tuition ("My parents still aren't sure how they feel about it," he says). He now owns twenty-seven dogs, which as you can imagine makes it somewhat tricky for him to obtain rental housing.

I was part of a two-sled party, which required eighteen dogs. A highlight of this experience—in fact, a highlight of my entire life—was watching Brian and his partner, Jeremy Gebauer, bring the dogs, one at a time, out of the truck. Because of course every single dog, immediately upon emerging, had to make weewee, and then every dog naturally had to sniff every other dog's weewee, which would cause the following thought to register in their primitive dog brains: "Hey! This is WEEWEE!" And so naturally this would cause every one of them to have to make MORE weewee, which every other one would of course have to sniff, the result being that we soon were witnessing what nuclear physicists call a Runaway Chain Weewee Reaction.

Eventually Brian and Jeremy got all the dogs into their harnesses, at which point they began to suspect that they might be about to run somewhere, which caused them to start barking at the rate of 250 barks per minute per dog.

I would estimate that at that moment our little group was responsible for two-thirds of the noise, and a solid three-quarters of the weewee, being produced in the western United States.

These dogs were *rarin'* to go. We passengers climbed into the sleds, and Brian and Jeremy stood on the runners behind. The sleds were tied firmly to the front bumper of the truck, but the dogs were pulling so hard that I swear I felt the truck move; I had this vision of us disappearing over the top of the mountain—dogs, followed by sleds, followed by truck, all headed for the Arctic Circle, never to be heard from again.

Quickly Brian and Jeremy untied the sleds and WHOOOAAAA we were off, whipping up the trail at a very brisk pace, the dogs insanely happy. Brian and Jeremy shouting traditional dog-team commands (my favorite traditional command, shouted by Brian, was: "BE NICE!").

These guys know their dogs; they watch them carefully and talk to them individually. Every dog runs a little differently, has a different personality. For example, on my sled's team, Sprocket was a good hard worker, a steady puller with a real nice gait; Brian hardly had to tell him anything. But he had to keep talking to Suzy, who was definitely not pulling her share of the load: She was more waddling than trotting. Brian would shout "SUZY!" and she'd start trotting for a while, but as soon as she thought he wasn't looking she'd go back to waddling. You could just tell that if Suzy worked for a large corporation, she'd spend most of her day making personal phone calls.

But most of the dogs were off to the races. In fact, the hard part is getting them to stop. Brian told us that one of the cardinal rules of this sport is that you never, ever get off and walk behind the sled.

"They'll leave you behind," he said.

We trotted briskly up to the top of the mountain, then Jeremy and Brian turned the sleds around in a maneuver that had all the smooth precision of a prison riot as the two teams of dogs suddenly decided this would be a good time for all eighteen of them to sniff each other's private regions. But they got straightened out, and we roared back down the hill; even Suzy was in overdrive. The sun was shining, the valley was spread out below us, the wind (not to mention the occasional whiff of dog poop) was whipping past our faces. It was a wonderful moment, and I felt as though I never wanted to get off the sled, even if there had been some way to stop it. I'll write when we reach Brazil.

SOMETHING IN THE AIR

When you're forty-seven years old, you sometimes hear a small voice inside you that says: "Just because you've reached middle age, that doesn't mean you shouldn't take on new challenges and seek new adventures. You get only one ride on this crazy carousel we call life, and by golly you should make the most of it!"

This is the voice of Satan.

I know this because recently, on a mountain in Idaho, I listened to this voice, and as a result my body feels as though it has been used as a trampoline by the Budweiser Clydesdales. I am currently on an all-painkiller diet. "I'll have a black coffee and 250 Advil tablets" is a typical breakfast order for me these days.

This is because I went snowboarding.

For those of you who, for whatever reason, such as a will to live, do not participate in downhill winter sports, I should explain that snowboarding is an activity that is very popular with people who do not feel that regular skiing is lethal enough. These are of course young people, fearless people, people with 100 percent synthetic bodies who can hurtle down a mountainside at fifty miles per hour and knock down mature trees with their faces and then spring to their feet and go, *"Cool."*

People like my son. He wanted to try snowboarding, and I thought it would be good to learn with him, because we can no longer ski together. We have a fundamental difference in technique: He skis via the Downhill Method, in which you ski down the hill; whereas I ski via the Breath-Catching Method, in which you stand sideways on the hill, looking as athletic as possible without actually moving muscles (this could cause you to start sliding down the hill). If anybody asks if you're okay, you say, "I'm just catching my breath!" in a tone of voice that suggests that at any moment you're going to swoop rapidly down the slope; whereas in fact you're planning to stay right where you are, rigid as a statue, until the spring thaw. At night, when the Downhillers have all gone home, we Breath-Catchers will still be up there, clinging to the mountainside, chewing on our parkas for sustenance.

So I thought I'd take a stab at snowboarding, which is quite different from skiing. In skiing, you wear a total of two skis, or approximately one per foot, so you can sort of maintain your balance by moving your feet, plus you have poles that you can stab people with if they make fun of you at close range. Whereas with snowboarding, all you get is one board, which is shaped like a giant tongue depressor and manufactured by the Institute of Extremely Slippery Things. Both of your feet are strapped firmly to this board, so that if you start to fall, you can't stick a foot out and catch yourself. You crash to the ground like a tree and lie there while skiers swoop past and deliberately spray snow on you.

Skiers hate snowboarders. It's a generational thing. Skiers are (and here I am generalizing) middle-aged Republicans wearing designer space suits; snowboarders are defiant young rebels wearing deliberately drab clothing that is baggy enough to contain the snowboarder plus a major appliance. Skiers like to glide down the slopes in a series of graceful arcs; snowboarders like to attack the mountain, slashing, spinning, tumbling, going backward, blasting through snow-drifts, leaping off cliffs, getting their noses pierced in midair, etc. Skiers view snowboarders as a menace; snowboarders view skiers as Elmer Fudd.

I took my snowboarding lesson in a small group led by a friend of mine named Brad Pearson, who also once talked me into jumping from a tall tree while attached only to a thin rope. Brad took us up on a slope that offered ideal snow conditions for the novice who's going to fall a lot: approximately seven flakes of powder on top of an eighteen-foot-thick base of reinforced concrete. You could not dent this snow with a jackhammer. (I later learned, however, that you *could* dent it with the back of your head.)

We learned snowboarding via a two-step method:

Step One: Watching Brad do something.

Step Two: Trying to do it ourselves.

I was pretty good at Step One. The problem with Step Two was that you had to stand up on your snowboard, which turns out to be a violation of at least five important laws of physics. I'd struggle to my feet, and I'd be wavering there and then the Physics Police would drop a huge chunk of gravity on me, and WHAM my body would hit the concrete snow, sometimes bouncing as much as a foot.

"Keep your knees bent!" Brad would yell helpfully. Have you noticed that whatever sport you're trying to learn, some earnest person is always telling you to keep your knees bent? As if THAT would solve anything. I wanted to shout back, "FORGET MY KNEES! DO SOMETHING ABOUT THESE GRAVITY CHUNKS!"

Needless to say my son had no trouble at all. None. In minutes he was cruising happily down the mountain; you could actually *see* his clothing getting baggier. I, on the other hand, spent most of my time lying on my back, groaning, while space-suited Republicans swooped past and sprayed snow on me. If I hadn't gotten out of there, they'd have completely covered me; I now realize that the small hills you see on ski slopes are formed around the bodies of forty-seven-year-olds who tried to learn snowboarding.

So I think, when my body heals, I'll go back to skiing. Maybe sometime you'll see me out on the slopes, catching my breath. Please throw me some food.

WHEEL OF MISFORTUNE

I f I had to summarize, in one sentence, the major lesson I have learned in life, that sentence would be: "Sometimes you have to buy a vowel."

I learned this lesson when I became a contestant on *Wheel of Fortune*, the hugely popular game show in which contestants try to figure out the hidden phrase, aided by the lovely and talented Vanna White, who smiles radiantly while turning over the letters one at a time. (Vanna, a total professional, could smile radiantly while having her spleen removed by weasels.)

The way I got on the show was, a *Wheel* staff person named Gary O'Brien, whose title is Talent Executive, sent me a letter asking me to participate in a special Award Winners' Week, to be taped in March and broadcast in May.

"Famous actors, actresses, directors, writers, singers, and sports stars will be spinning the famous Wheel for their favorite charities," Gary wrote.

I said I'd do it, and not just because I like to benefit charity by hanging around with famous actors and actresses. I also happen to be very good at word games, particularly the part where you cheat. You should see me play Scrabble.

Me (forming a word): *There!*
My Opponent: *"Doot?" There's no such word as "doot."*
Me (offended): *Of COURSE there is. It's an infarctive gerund.*
My Opponent (skeptically): *Use it in a sentence.*
Me: *"Look! A doot!"*
My Opponent: *Oh, okay.*

So I figured, how hard could *Wheel of Fortune* be? Whenever I've watched the show, the hidden phrase has always seemed pathetically easy to figure out. Some contestant will be staring at the big board, sweating bullets, trying to make sense of some letters and blanks arranged like this:

- - N - - - - - - - - N - - R - - - M -

I'll look at this for two seconds, then shout at the screen, "It's OBVIOUS, you moron! HUNCHBACK OF NOTRE DAME!"

I bet you do the same thing. We all do. Each day 24 million people watch *Wheel of Fortune,* and every single one of them always figures out the hidden phrase before the actual contestants do.

But after I agreed to be on the show, I began to have second thoughts. I realized that it's probably WAY harder to solve the puzzle when you're under the hot studio lights, in front of cameras and a live studio audience, with Pat Sajak standing right there and Vanna beaming high-intensity smile rays right at you from close range.

So as the date of my taping approached, I worked on my *Wheel* strategy. I started asking everybody I talked to, including Directory Assistance, whether I should buy a vowel. Unfortunately, there was no consensus on this issue. Some people said yes, definitely; some said no, absolutely not, never buy a vowel. The only real expert I consulted was a United Airlines ticket agent named Rico, whom I met at Dulles airport when I was catching a flight to Los Angeles to be on the show. Rico told me that he had actually been a winning contestant on *Wheel of Fortune.*

"Should I buy a vowel?" I asked him.

"Not unless you really need it," replied Rico helpfully.

In Los Angeles I was taken to the *Wheel* TV studio by an Iranian limousine driver named Max, who was deeply impressed by my enormous fame and celebrity.

"So, Mr. David," he said. "You are a singer?"

"No," I said. "Should I buy a vowel?"

"Yes," said Max. "You have to."

At the studio I met some of the other famous celebrities participating in Award Winners' Week, including rap artist and actor "L.L. Cool J." (That is not his real name, of course. His real name is "L.L. Cool M.") I also met the two celebrities I would be competing against, actresses Rita Moreno and Justine Miceli.

Gary, the Talent Executive, gave us a briefing on how to play the game; this briefing consisted almost entirely of detailed instructions on how to spin the wheel.

"Make sure your hand is dry," Gary said. "Reach as far to the right as you can, get a good grip on the upper part of the spoke, and then pull."

We all practiced spinning the wheel and calling out consonants, although some celebrities, unfamiliar with the rules, tried to call out vowels.

"You have to *buy* a vowel," Gary said, several times. "Once you spin, you're committed to calling a consonant."

When all of us celebrities were fairly confident that we didn't have a clue what was going on, the live studio audience was brought in, and we began taping. In the interest of drama I am not going to reveal the outcome of my game, which has not aired yet, except to say, in all modesty, that I did get to the Bonus Round, where I had ten seconds to try to solve the following phrase:

- OME - O L - - E

You have no idea how truly stupid you can feel until you try to guess a hidden phrase in front of a live studio audience—every single member of which, you are convinced, knows the answer. For ten seemingly endless seconds, sounding like a person with some kind of language-related brain malfunction, you blurt out random incorrect answers ("HOME TO LOVE!" "ROME TO LIVE!" "NOME NO LIKE!" "DOME SO . . .")

Of course I'm sure that you, Mr. or Ms. Smarty Pants Reader, immediately figured out the right answer, which is: "SOME DO DOOT."

No, really, I'm sure you solved it. If not, you should watch the show. Or you can contact me. If you play your cards right, maybe I'll sell you a vowel.

THIS ONE WILL KILL YOU

I really didn't want to get into another fight with the classical-music people.

Awhile back I wrote a column in which I was mildly critical of classical music on the grounds that it sucks and I hate it. Rather than respond to these arguments on their intellectual merits, many classical-music fans responded with snotty personal attacks in which they suggested that I am the kind of cultural moron who sits around all day watching TV with a beer in one hand and the remote control in the other. This is a lie. Sometimes I have beers in BOTH hands, forcing me to operate the remote control with my feet.

No, seriously, I happen to be a highly cultured individual. I have been involved in tour groups that walked briskly past some of the world's finest works of art. I personally own several hardcover books and have read *The Cat in the Hat Comes Back* out loud at least 400 times. I am perfectly comfortable ordering food in a swank French restaurant ("Mr. Garçon, I'll have the beef *en route*").

In short, I have culture out the wazoo. I just have never cared for classical music, because I believe that the artistic themes it embodies are not presented in a manner that is intellectually relevant for the modern listener. Take, for example, the following actual unretouched lyrics, written by Lorenzo da Ponte for the Mozart opera *Cosi Fan Tutte* (literally, *Annie Get Your Gun*):

Che sembianze! Che vestiti!
Che figure! Che mustacchi!

After carefully analyzing these lyrics, the objective critic is forced to arrive at one incontrovertible conclusion: *They are written in a completely foreign language*, probably Spanish. You have to ask yourself how in the world these opera people expected to reach a modern audience if they didn't even have the common courtesy to write in English. Compare the seemingly deliberate impenetrability of their lyrics with the inviting clarity of the 1964 song "Mammer Jammer," in which Don and Dewey, exploring the complex depths of human relationships, state:

You got to do the Mammer Jammer
If you want my love.

Please do not misunderstand me: I am not saying that people cannot enjoy opera. I am just saying that these people are wrong. They also could be in big medical trouble. I base this statement on an Associated Press article, sent in by many alert readers, concerning an alarming incident in Denmark involving an okapi, which is a rare African mammal related to the giraffe. The article states that this okapi—I am not making this quotation up—"died from stress apparently triggered by opera singers."

The okapi was not actually attending an opera when this happened. It was in a zoo located 300 yards from a park where opera singers were rehearsing. A zoo spokesperson was quoted as saying that okapis "can be severely affected by unusual sounds."

So here are the essential facts:

1. An okapi, minding its own business, was killed by opera music being sung *three football fields away.*
2. Okapis are members of the mammal family.
3. Most human beings, not counting Congress, are also members of the mammal family.

When I consider these facts together, a very disturbing question comes to my mind, as I'm sure it does yours: *What were three football fields doing in Denmark?*

Another question is: Could opera, in sufficient dosages, also be fatal to human beings? The only way to find out is to conduct a scientific experiment, in which we would take a group of volunteer subjects—and as the person proposing this experiment, I am willing to courageously volunteer that these subjects be scientists from the Tobacco Institute—strap them into chairs, and blast opera at them twenty-four hours a day until such time as they are dead.

Of course to ensure that this experiment was scientifically valid, we'd also need what is known technically as a "control"; this would be a second group of volunteer Tobacco Institute scientists, who would be strapped into chairs and blasted with some *other* kind of music. I am thinking here of the Neil Diamond Christmas album.

Once this experiment had proved scientifically that opera music is fatal, it would be time to think about requiring that some kind of Surgeon General warning be prominently displayed on Luciano Pavarotti. Also we'd have to study the effects of "secondhand opera," which is what you get when inconsiderate individuals start humming opera music in a poorly ventilated office, and suddenly their coworkers are dropping like flies, especially if their coworkers happen to be okapis.

Ultimately, we may have to ban opera altogether, along with—you can't take chances with the public health—ballet, nonrhyming poetry, movies with subtitles, and any kind of sculpture that does not accurately depict naked women. I realize that, for taking this stand, I'm going to be harshly criticized by the so-called cultured crowd. But I frankly cannot worry about that, because I have the courage of my convictions. Also, *Inspector Gadget* is on.

THE FAT LADY SINGS

My advice to you, if you ever get invited to play the part of a corpse in an opera, is: *Ask questions.* Here are some that I would suggest:

1. Does the plot of this opera call for the corpse to get shoved halfway off a bed headfirst by people shrieking in Italian?
2. If so, is this corpse wearing a nightgown-style garment that could easily get bunched up around the corpse's head if the corpse finds itself in an inverted position with its legs sticking up in the air on a brightly lit stage in front of hundreds of people whom the corpse does not personally know?
3. If so, what, if any, provisions will be made to prevent a public viewing of the corpse's butt?

Fool that I am, I failed to ask these questions when I was invited to be a deceased person in an opera. This invitation resulted from a column I wrote concerning an animal in a Denmark zoo that died from stress brought on by hearing opera singers rehearse. I concluded that opera is probably fatal and should be banned as a public-health menace, just like heroin, or aspirin bottles with lids that can actually be opened.

This column generated a large amount of mail from irate opera lovers who:

1. Pointed out that they are far more sophisticated, urbane, and cultured than I am, and
2. Used some really dirty words.

(Here is an actual quote from one of these letters, slightly modified for the family-newspaper audience: "*Cosi Fan Tutte* is Italian and not Spanish, you sock plucker. Duck shoe.")

But I also got a very nice letter from Janice Mackey, general manager of Eugene Opera in Eugene, Oregon (civic motto: "Eventually You Stop Noticing the Rain"). She invited me to play a corpse in Eugene Opera's January 8 performance of *Gianni Schicchi* (pronounced "Johnny SKEE-kee"), a work by the famous opera dude Puccini ("Poo-CHEE-nee"), who I believe also wrote the 1966 Tommy James hit "Hanky Panky" ("Hang-kee PANG-kee"). As a professional journalist, I am always looking for new ways to get paid for being motionless, so I said sure.

Eugene is located in southwest Oregon, approximately 278 billion miles from anything. To get there, you have to take a series of "commuter" airplanes, each one smaller than the last, until finally there isn't room for both you and the pilot, and you have to fly yourself. "Eugene is that way!" the airline personnel tell you, gesturing vaguely. "Just look for the rain cloud!"

But Eugene Opera turned out to be a very professional outfit featuring baritones, sopranos, bassoons, tremors, mezzanines, etc. I attended a brief rehearsal, during which the professional opera singers practiced shoving me off the bed and gave me invaluable dramatic tips on playing dead ("Don't move"). They also filled me in on the plot of *Gianni Schicchi*, which involves a wealthy thirteenth-century Florentine named Buoso Donati, who is pursued by a seemingly indestructible android from the future.

No, wait, that's the plot of *Terminator II*. The plot of *Gianni Schicchi* is that Buoso is dead, and a bunch of people sing very loudly about this in Italian for 45 minutes of opera time, which, for a normal human, works out to roughly a month. I spent most of this time lying still on the bed with my mouth open. This turns out to be very difficult. When you have to hold perfectly still in front of hundreds of people, you become a seething mass of primitive bodily needs. You develop overpowering urges to swallow, twitch, scratch, burp, emit vapors, and—above all—lick your lips. "YOU NEED TO LICK YOUR LIPS RIGHT NOW!" is the urgent message your brain repeatedly sends to your tongue. You find yourself abandoning all concerns about personal hygiene and praying that Puccini was thoughtful enough to include a part in *Gianni Schicchi* where the singers decide, for whatever reason, to lick the corpse's lips.

But this is not what happens. What happens is that the singers, while searching for Buoso's will, shove the corpse off the bed, the result being that I had to hold perfectly still while upside down, with my face smushed into a low footstool and my legs in the air, through several arias ("aria" is Italian for "song that will not end in your lifetime"). Fortunately, under my nightgown I was wearing tights, so the audience was never directly exposed to my butt, which could have triggered a potentially deadly stampede for the exits.

Finally the singers put the corpse back up on the bed, so for the rest of the opera I could just lie there thinking explicit bodily thoughts. At times I also listened to the music, and I have to say that, although I am by no means an opera aficionado (literally, "guy"), I was deeply moved by one part, which was when a stagehand, Doug Beebe, crept up behind my bed, unseen by the audience, and whispered, "Dolphins 21, Chargers 8." He was updating me on an important NFL playoff game in which I had a strong artistic interest. And although the Dolphins ultimately lost, I definitely enjoyed performing in *Gianni Schicchi* and did not find the experience to be the least bit fatal, so I sincerely apologize to all the opera fans I offended.

Except for the gas poles who wrote the nasty letters.

BORRRINNNG!

Ⅰ was at an airport, reading a newspaper, when the World's Three Most Boring People sat down next to me and started talking as loud as they could without amplifiers. They were so boring I took notes on their conversation. Here's an actual excerpt:

> *First Person (pointing to a big bag): That's a big bag.*
> *Second Person: That* is *a big bag.*
> *First Person: You can hold a lot in a bag like that.*
> *Third Person: Francine has a big bag like that.*
> *First Person: Francine does? Like that?*
> *Third Person: Yes. It holds everything. She puts everything in that bag.*
> *Second Person: It's a big bag.*
> *Third Person: She says whatever she has, she just puts it in that bag and just boom, closes it up.*
> *First Person: Francine does?*
> *Second Person: That is a big bag.*

I want to stress that this was not all that they had to say about the big bag. They could have gone on for hours if they hadn't been interrupted by a major news development:

namely, a person walking past pulling a wheeled suitcase. This inspired a whole new train of thought: ("There's one of those suitcases with those wheels." "Where?" "There, with those wheels." "John has one." "He does?" "With those wheels?" "Yes. He says you just roll it along." "John does?")

And so on. It occurred to me that a possible explanation for some plane crashes might be that people like these were sitting close enough to the cockpit for the flight crew to hear them talk ("There's a cloud." "Look, there's *another* . . .") and eventually the pilot deliberately flies into the ground to make them shut up.

The thing is, these people clearly didn't know they were boring. Boring people never do. In fact, no offense, even YOU could be boring. Ask yourself: When you talk to people, do they tend to make vague excuses—"Sorry! Got to run!"—and then walk briskly away? Does this happen even if you are in an elevator?

But even if people listen to you with what appears to be great interest, that doesn't mean you're not boring. They could be pretending. When Prince Charles speaks, everybody pretends to be fascinated, even though he has never said anything interesting except in that intercepted telephone conversation wherein he expressed the desire to be a feminine hygiene product.

And even if you're not Prince Charles, people might have to pretend you're interesting because they want to sell you something, or have intimate carnal knowledge of you, or because you hold some power over them. At one time I was a co-investor in a small aging apartment building with plumbing and electrical systems that were brought over on the *Mayflower;* my partner and I were regularly visited by the building inspector, who had the power to write us up for numerous minor building-code infractions, which is why we always pretended to be fascinated when he told us—as he ALWAYS did—about the time he re-plumbed his house. His account of this event was as long as *The Iliad*, but with more soldering. I'm sure he told this story to everybody whose building he ever inspected; he's probably still telling it, unless some building owner finally strangled him, in which case I bet his wife never reported that he was missing.

The point is that you could easily be unaware that you're boring. This is why everybody should make a conscious effort to avoid boring topics. The problem here, of course, is that not everybody agrees on what "boring" means. For example, Person A might believe that collecting decorative plates is boring, whereas Person B might find this to be a fascinating hobby. Who's to say which person is correct?

I am. Person A is correct. Plate-collecting is boring. In fact, hobbies of any kind are boring except to people who have the same hobby. (This is also true of religion, although you will not find me saying so in print.) The New Age is boring, and so are those puzzles where you try to locate all the hidden words. Agriculture is important but boring. Likewise foreign policy. Also, come to think of it, domestic policy. The fact that your child made the honor roll is boring. Auto racing is boring except when a car is going at least 172 miles per hour upside down. Talking about golf is always boring. (*Playing* golf can be interesting, but not the part where you try to hit the little ball; only the part where you drive the cart.) Fishing is boring, unless you catch an actual fish, and then it is disgusting.

Speaking of sports, a big problem is that men and women often do not agree on what is boring. Men can devote an entire working week to discussing a single pass-interference penalty; women find this boring, yet can be fascinated by a four-hour movie with subtitles wherein the entire plot consists of a man and a woman yearning to have, but never actually having, a relationship. Men HATE that. Men can take maybe 45 seconds of yearning, and then they want everybody to get naked. Followed by a car chase. A movie called *Naked People in Car Chases* would do really well among men. I have quite a few more points to make, but I'm sick of this topic.

LET'S DO LUNCH

I am not one to drop names, but I was recently invited to a private luncheon with Hillary Rodham Clinton, First Lady of the Whole Entire United States.

This is true. I got the invitation from Mrs. Clinton's office, and I said that heck yes, I would go. I will frankly admit that I was excited. Mrs. Clinton would be the most important federal human with whom I have ever privately luncheoned.

I did once attend a dinner with Richard "Dick" Cheney when he was the secretary of defense under President George "Herbert Walker" Bush, but that was not a one-on-one situation. That was at the Cartoonists' Dinner at the *Washington Post,* an annual event wherein political cartoonists get a chance to come out from behind their drawing boards and, in an informal setting with high-level federal officials, make fools of themselves. At least that's what generally happens. I am not one to generalize, but cartoonists, as a group, exhibit a level of social sophistication generally associated with pie fights. In high school, when the future lawyers were campaigning for class president, the future cartoonists were painstakingly altering illustrations in their history books so that Robert E. Lee appeared to be performing an illegal act with his horse.

So the Cartoonists' Dinner usually provides some entertaining interaction between cartoonists and Washington dignitaries, such as the time a couple of years ago when a cartoonist, doing a heartfelt impersonation of Elvis in concert giving away a Cadillac, hurled a set of car keys behind his back, through the air, directly into the forehead of the wife of a Cabinet official. She took this graciously, but you could tell that henceforth she was going to stick to cartoonist-free gatherings.

As a maturity-impaired individual, I have had the honor of being invited to the Cartoonists' Dinner on several occasions, which, as I mentioned, is how I came to meet Dick Cheney. I actually met him about six times. You know those situations where you have consumed a few unnecessary beers and think you're being the funniest thing on two feet, whereas in fact you're just being stupid? This was one of those situations. We were mingling before dinner, and for reasons that I cannot explain now, whenever I encountered Cheney, which was fairly often because this was a smallish room, I'd thrust out my hand and say, "Hi, Dick! Dave Barry!" There he was, the secretary of defense, probably trying to think about the Persian Gulf, and every 45 seconds he was shaking hands with the same grinning moron. It's a good thing I didn't have car keys.

But humiliating yourself in front of the secretary of defense, as impressive as it is, is not on a par with being invited to a private luncheon with the first lady. I was especially eager to share my views on health care, assuming I could think some up. Also I wanted to find out what it was like to be a first lady. Once, at a dinner, I sat next to a very funny first lady of a large state that shall remain nameless. She told me that she and some other governors' wives had once come up with the idea of getting lifesize smiling photographs of themselves and mounting them on pieces of cardboard to be used as portable first ladies. Thus the real first lady could have a life, while the portable one would be carried around to political events and propped up behind the governor.

"That's all they really need to represent us," the governor's wife told me, "because all we ever do is stand there and smile, and they introduce the governor, and then they say, 'And here is his lovely wife.' That's what they always say, 'Here is his lovely wife,' even if she is actually a dog."

So we see that first ladies can be pretty entertaining, and I was fired up about my impending luncheon with Mrs. Clinton. We had set a date and a time, and everything seemed set—until Mrs. Clinton's staff person, Lisa Caputo, informed me that the luncheon was going to be "off the record." I asked what that meant.

"Mrs. Clinton would like to meet you," Caputo said. "This is a chance for you to get together and have a good time. But you can't write about it."

My crest fell when I heard those words, because I knew I could not accept this restriction. I am a professional journalist, and if I'm going to have luncheon with one of this nation's most powerful political figures, then I feel a deep moral obligation to provide you, my readers, with an irresponsible and highly distorted account of it.

I explained this to Caputo, but it was no use; either the luncheon had to be off the record, or there would be no luncheon. So there was no luncheon. I think this is a shame, because I bet it would have been a fun occasion, possibly culminating, if we really hit it off, in my showing the first lady how to make comical hand noises. So in closing, I want to say: Mrs. Clinton, if you're reading this, I sincerely appreciate the invitation, and I'm sorry it didn't work out, and someday I hope we can sit down and have fun on the record, and if it would make you feel more comfortable, you're certainly welcome to also invite you-know-who (Dick Cheney).

THE LOBSTER
REBELLION

I am pleased to report that the scientific community has finally stopped wasting time on the origins of the universe and started dealing with the important question, which is: Are lobsters really just big insects?

I have always maintained that they are. I personally see no significant difference between a lobster and, say, a giant Madagascar hissing cockroach, which is a type of cockroach that grows to approximately the size of William Howard Taft (1857–1930). If a group of diners were sitting in a nice restaurant, and the waiter were to bring them each a freshly killed, steaming-hot Madagascar hissing cockroach, they would not put on silly bibs and eat it with butter. No, they would run, retching, directly from the restaurant to the All-Nite Drive-Thru Lawsuit Center. And yet these very same people will pay $24.95 apiece to eat a lobster, despite the fact that it displays all three of the classic biological characteristics of an insect, namely:

1. It has way more legs than necessary.
2. There is no way you would ever pet it.

3. It does not respond to simple commands such as "Here, boy!"

I do not eat lobsters, although I once had a close call. I was visiting my good friends Tom and Pat Schroth, who live in Maine (state motto: "Cold, but Damp"). Being generous and hospitable people, Tom and Pat went out and purchased, as a special treat for me, the largest lobster in the history of the Atlantic Ocean, a lobster that had probably been responsible for sinking many commercial vessels before it was finally apprehended by nuclear submarines. This lobster was big enough to feed a coastal Maine village for a year, and there it was, sprawling all over my plate, with scary insectoid legs and eyeballs shooting out in all directions, while Tom and Pat, my gracious hosts, smiled happily at me, waiting for me to put this thing in my mouth.

Remember when you were a child, and your mom wouldn't let you leave the dinner table until you ate all your Brussels sprouts, and so you took your fork and mashed them into smaller and smaller pieces in hopes of eventually reducing them to individual Brussels-sprout molecules that would be absorbed into the atmosphere and disappear? That was similar to the approach I took with the giant lobster.

"Mmmm-MMMM!" I said, hacking away at the thing on my plate and, when nobody was looking, concealing the pieces under my dinner roll, in the salad, in my napkin, anywhere I could find.

Tom and Pat: I love you dearly, and if you should ever have an electrical problem that turns out to be caused by a seven-pound wad of old lobster pieces stuffed into the dining-room wall socket, I am truly sorry.

Anyway, my point is that lobsters have long been suspected, by me at least, of being closet insects, which is why I was very pleased recently when my alert journalism colleague Steve Doig referred me to an Associated Press article concerning a discovery by scientists at the University of Wisconsin. The article, headlined GENE LINKS SPIDERS AND FLIES TO LOBSTERS, states that not only do lobsters, flies, spiders, millipedes, etc., contain *the exact same gene*, but they also are all descended from a single common ancestor: Howard Stern.

No, seriously, the article states that the ancestor "probably was a wormlike creature." Yum! Fetch the melted butter!

And that is not all. According to articles sent in by alert readers (this was on the *front page* of the *New York Times*), scientists in Denmark recently discovered that some lobsters have a weird little pervert organism living *on their lips*. Yes. I didn't even know that lobsters HAD lips, but it turns out that they do, and these lips are the stomping ground of a tiny creature called *Symbion pandora* (literally, "a couple of Greek words"). The zoology community, which does not get out a lot, is extremely excited about *Symbion pandora*, because it reproduces differently from all other life forms. According to various articles, when *Symbion pandora* is ready to have a baby, its digestive system "collapses and is reconstituted into a larva," which the parent then gives birth to by "extruding" it from its "posterior." In other words—correct me if I am wrong here—this thing basically reproduces by pooping.

So to summarize: If you're looking for a hearty entrée that (1) is related to spiders; (2) is descended from a worm; and (3) has mutant baby-poopers walking around on its lips, then you definitely want a lobster. I myself plan to continue avoiding them, just as I avoid oysters, which are clearly—scientists should look into this next—members of the phlegm family. Have you ever seen oysters reproduce? Neither have I, but I would not be surprised to learn that the process involves giant undersea nostrils.

And don't get me started on clams. Recently I sat across from a person who was deliberately eating clams; she'd open up a shell, and there, in plain view, would be this stark naked clam, brazenly showing its organs, like a high school biology experiment. My feeling is that if a restaurant is going to serve those things, it should put little loincloths on them.

I believe that Mother Nature gave us eyes because she did not want us to eat this type of food. Mother Nature clearly intended for us to get our food from the "patty" group, which includes hamburgers, fish sticks, and McNuggets—foods that have had all of their organs safely removed in someplace far away such as Nebraska. That is where I stand on this issue, and if any qualified member of the lobster, clam, or phlegm-in-a-shell industry wishes to present a rebuttal, I hereby extend this offer: Get your own column.

ANIMAL RIGHTS

A question that more and more Americans are asking, as they become increasingly fed up with crime, is: What, exactly, are the legal rights of accused snakes?

Consider the case of a snake that recently ran afoul of the law in Virginia. According to a story in the Fredericksburg, Virginia, *Free Lance-Star,* written by Keith Epps and sent in by alert reader Venetia Sims, this particular snake, a four-foot Burmese python identified only as "a Spotsylvania County snake," was apprehended by an Alcoholic Beverage Control agent and the Spotsylvania Sheriff's Office in connection with a liquor-store robbery.

I am not, of course, suggesting here that the police thought the snake ROBBED the store. They thought it drove the getaway car.

No, seriously, the snake belonged to one of the robbery suspects, and according to the story the police had received information that the snake had money from the robbery "stashed inside of it."

The story doesn't say how a person would go about stashing money inside a snake, nor how this person would get the money back out. But for the record, most financial advisers do not recommend that you put your money into snakes. Let me add, from personal experience, that real estate is not such a hot investment either. Some friends and I once put some money into a small apartment building, and we never did get it back out. What we got was a constant stream of tenant complaints, including every conceivable kind of toilet blockage and—this is the absolute truth—an infestation of bats that made the local TV news. Looking back, I think we would have been better off with a snake.

But getting back to "a Spotsylvania County snake": The police took it into custody (presumably in a handcuff) and held it without bail for a week, during which time they X-rayed it. According to the story, the X ray "revealed something suspicious inside the snake, but police weren't sure what it was." It turned out to be snake poop, which—and this is exactly what is wrong with our society today, if you want my and Pat Buchanan's opinion—is still legal in Virginia.

So the police were forced to release the snake, although NOT on its own recognizance. (One of the unique things about snakes is that they don't even HAVE a recognizance; biologists still have no idea how they reproduce.)

At this point you are saying: "Dave, no offense, but it is just SO typical of media scum like you to make a big deal about one snake who is connected to a liquor-store robbery, while totally ignoring the millions of law-abiding, taxpaying snakes, not to mention ferrets."

You make a strong point, which is why at this time I wish to present an inspiring story, which I am not making up, concerning a courageous ferret in Morton Grove, Illinois. According to an item from the *Northbrook Star*, written by Kathy Routliffe and alertly sent in by Janet Kolehmainen, police received an emergency 911 call from a home in Morton Grove; upon arriving on the scene, they broke into the home and discovered that the call had been made by a pet ferret named "Bandit."

Unfortunately, this did not turn out to be one of those heartwarming cases wherein a loyal and quick-thinking ferret, seeing that its master was having a heart attack, called police and then administered snout-to-mouth resuscitation until help arrived. This was simply a case of Bandit, while walking around the house alone, stepping on the telephone speed-dial button for 911. But the point is that there *could* have been a medical problem, and if there had, Bandit would be a hero today, perhaps even making a personal appearance on the *Jerry Springer* show.

Speaking of crustaceans, it's time for a:

Lobster Update—I have been deeply gratified by the tremendous outpouring of letters from you readers supporting my courageous decision to come out of the closet and state that I think lobsters are big insects. Some of you also sent me an alarming news item stating that researchers at Harvard Medical School are—I swear I'm not making this up, either—giving Prozac to lobsters. The researchers say the drug "makes lobsters more docile, and less likely to snap when fished out of a tank at a restaurant."

The article states that the researchers hope their work will ultimately benefit humans. This raises some alarming questions:

1. Are there restaurants that keep humans in tanks?
2. Are these humans forced to wear rubber bands on their hands?
3. Do the restaurant owners claim that they taste "just like chicken"?

I think that every concerned American should telephone federal authorities at random until we get answers to these and other questions. I also think that, for the time being, we should all be extremely cautious when we leave our homes. Remember: "a Spotsylvania County snake" is out there somewhere.

Here I am performing the difficult "Walking the Dog" maneuver with the Lawn Rangers, a world-famous precision lawnmower-and-broom drill team to which I belong. We perform each year at the Arcola, Illinois, Broom Corn Festival. Our membership ranks are strictly limited to anybody who shows up. *(Photo by David H. Spencer)*

OUR NATIONAL PASTIME

As I ponder the start of yet another baseball season, what is left of my mind drifts back to the fall of 1960, when I was a student at Harold C. Crittenden Junior High ("Where the Leaders of Tomorrow Are Developing the Acne of Today").

The big baseball story that year was the World Series between the New York Yankees and the Pittsburgh Pirates. Today, for sound TV viewership reasons, all World Series games are played after most people, including many of the players, have gone to bed. But in 1960 the games had to be played in the daytime, because the electric light had not been invented yet. Also, back then the players and owners had not yet discovered the marketing benefits of sporadically canceling entire seasons.

The result was that in those days young people were actually interested in baseball, unlike today's young people, who are much more interested in basketball, football, soccer, and downloading dirty pictures from the Internet. But in my youth, baseball ruled. Almost all of us boys played in

Little League, a character-building experience that helped me develop a personal relationship with God.

"God," I would say, when I was standing in deep right field—the coach put me in right field only because it was against the rules to put me in Sweden, where I would have done less damage to the team—"please please PLEASE don't let the ball come to me."

But of course God enjoys a good prank as much as the next infallible deity, which is why, when He heard me pleading with Him, He always took time out from His busy schedule to make sure the next batter hit a towering blast that would, upon reentering the Earth's atmosphere, come down directly where I would have been standing, if I had stood still, which I never did. I lunged around cluelessly in frantic, random circles, so that the ball always landed a minimum of forty feet from where I wound up standing, desperately thrusting out my glove, which was a Herb Score model that, on my coach's recommendation, I had treated with neat's-foot oil so it would be supple. Looking back, I feel bad that innocent neats had to sacrifice their feet for the sake of my glove. I would have been just as effective, as a fielder, if I'd been wearing a bowling shoe on my hand, or a small aquarium.

But even though I stunk at it, I was into baseball. My friends and I collected baseball cards, the kind that came in a little pack with a dusty, pale-pink rectangle of linoleum-textured World War II surplus bubble gum that was far less edible than the cards themselves. Like every other male my age who collected baseball cards as a boy, I now firmly believe that at one time I had the original rookie cards of Mickey Mantle, Jackie Robinson, Ty Cobb, Babe Ruth, Jim Thorpe, Daniel Boone, Goliath, etc., and that I'd be able to sell my collection for $163 million today except my mom threw it out.

My point is that we cared deeply about baseball back then, which meant that we were passionate about the 1960 Pirates-Yankees World Series matchup. My class was evenly divided between those who were Pirate fans and those who were complete morons. (I never have cared for the Yankees, and for a very sound reason: The Yankees are evil.)

We followed every pitch of every game. It wasn't easy, because the weekday games started when we were still in school, which for some idiot reason was not called off for the World Series. This meant that certain students—I am not naming names, because even now, it could go on our Permanent Records—had to carry concealed transistor radios to class. A major reason why the Russians got so far ahead of us, academically, during the Cold War is that while Russian students were listening to their teachers explain the cosine, we were listening, via concealed earphones, to announcers explain how a bad hop nailed Tony Kubek in the throat.

That Series went seven games, and I vividly remember how it ended. School was out for the day, and I was heading home, pushing my bike up a steep hill, listening to my cheapo little radio, my eyes staring vacantly ahead, my mind locked on the game. A delivery truck came by, and the driver stopped and asked if he could listen. Actually, he more or less *told* me he was going to listen; I said okay.

The truck driver turned out to be a rabid Yankee fan. The game was very close, and we stood on opposite sides of my bike for the final two innings, rooting for opposite teams, him chain-smoking Lucky Strike cigarettes, both of us hanging on every word coming out of my tinny little speaker.

And of course if you were around back then and did not live in Russia, you know what happened: God, in a sincere effort to make up for all those fly balls he directed toward me in Little League, had Bill Mazeroski—Bill Mazeroski!—hit a home run to win it for the Pirates.

I was insane with joy. The truck driver was devastated. But I will never forget what he said to me. He looked me square in the eye, one baseball fan to another, after a tough but fair fight—and he said a seriously bad word. Several, in fact. Then he got in his truck and drove away.

That was the best game I ever saw.

HERE COMES THE BRIDE

We're coming into wedding season, a magical time when the radiant bride, on her Most Special Day, finally makes that long-awaited walk down the Aisle of Joyfulness to stand next to the Man of Her Dreams, only to sprint back up the Aisle of Joyfulness when she suddenly realizes that she forgot to pluck out her Middle Eyebrow Hairs of Grossness. Because the bride knows that a wedding video is forever. She knows that, twenty years later, she could be showing her video to friends, and as soon as she left the room they'd turn to each other and say, "What was that on her forehead? A tarantula?"

Oh yes, there is a LOT of pressure on today's bride to make her Big Day fabulous and perfect. Overseeing a modern wedding is comparable, in terms of complexity, to flying the Space Shuttle; in fact it's *worse,* because shuttle crew members don't have to select their silver pattern. This is done for them by ground-based engineers:

Command Center: Okay, Discovery, *we're gonna go with the "Fromage de Poisson" pattern, over?*

Discovery: Houston, we have a problem with the asparagus server.

Of course the bride does get some help. The multibillion-dollar U.S. wedding industry—currently the second-largest industry in the United States, behind the *latte* industry—helps the bride by publishing monthly bridal magazines the size of the U.S. tax code full of products that the bride absolutely HAS to have and checklists relentlessly reminding the bride of all the decisions she has to make RIGHT NOW concerning critical issues such as the florist and the caterer and the cake and the centerpieces and the guest favors for the formal cocktail reception. (Of COURSE there have to be guest favors at the formal cocktail reception! Don't you know ANYTHING?)

Of course the groom has responsibilities, too. According to ancient tradition, on the morning of the wedding the groom must check the TV listings to make sure that there is no playoff game scheduled during the ceremony, because if there is, he would have to miss it (the ceremony).

But the other 19 million wedding details are pretty much left up to the bride; this is why, when she finally gets to her Most Special Day, she is clinically insane. Exhibit A is Princess Diana. People ask: "What went wrong? Princess Diana had the Fairy Tale Wedding of the Century!" Yes! Exactly! YOU try planning the Fairy Tale Wedding of the Century! This poor woman didn't just have to think about party favors; she had HORSES in her wedding. A LOT of them. Just try to imagine the etiquette issues: What color should the horses be? Should they be invited to the reception? Should they have centerpieces? What if they *eat* the centerpieces? These are just a few of the issues Princess Diana was grappling with while Prince Charles was out riding around whacking grouse with a polo mallet. No wonder there was tension!

But it's not just Princess Diana: Wedding planning makes *all* brides crazy. Anybody who doubts this statement should investigate what actually goes on at a "bridal shower." I don't know about you, but I used to think that a shower was just a sedate little party wherein the bride's women friends gave thoughtful little gifts to the bride and ate salads with low-fat dressing on the side. Wrong! You would not *believe* the bizarre things women do at these affairs. For example, I have it on excellent authority that women at showers play this game wherein teams compete to see who can make the best wedding dress *out of toilet paper.* I'm not making this up! Ask a shower attendee! If a *man* were to wrap himself in a personal hygiene product, he'd immediately be confined in a room with no sharp objects, but this is considered normal behavior for a woman planning a wedding.

I have been informed by an informed source that women at bridal showers also sometimes play a variation of "Pin the Tail on the Donkey," except that instead of a picture of a donkey, they use a picture of a man, and instead of a tail, they use something that is not a tail, if you get my drift. I am not suggesting that Princess Diana played this game at her shower, and I am certainly not suggesting that the Queen did, so just get that mental picture out of your mind right now.

All I'm saying is that, with spring upon us, you may find yourself near a woman in the throes of planning a wedding; if so, you need to recognize that she is under severe pressure, and above all you need to do *exactly as she says.* If she wants you to wrap yourself in toilet paper, or purchase and wear a bridesmaid's dress that makes you look like a walking Barcalounger, JUST DO IT. You should do it even if you are the groom. Because this is the bride's Most Special Day, and you want to help her make sure everything is exactly the way you want it when the two of you finally stand together in front of all your friends and loved ones, and you gaze upon her face, and you say the words she has been waiting a lifetime to hear: "Hey! What's that between your eyebrows?"

THE CIGAR AVENGER

Just when you're starting to lose hope that the younger generation will ever amount to anything; just when you're asking yourself, "Where are the leaders of tomorrow? Where is the next John Kennedy, the next John Wayne, the next John Denver, the next John LeMasters, who attended Pleasantville High School with me and was very good at math?"; just when you're starting to think that the most significant contributions that today's young people will make to society will be in the field of body-piercing; just when you're about to give up in total despair, some young person, when you least expect it, sends you a world-class water gun.

At least that's what happened to me. The young person in this case is actually named John Young. He's a graduate student who wrote me a letter informing me that several years earlier, while sitting in a philosophy class—and let this be a lesson to you students who think that studying philosophy is a waste of time—he figured out how to make "the most butt-kickingest water gun the world has ever seen."

He calls it the Ultimate Water Gun, and when he offered to let me try it, I of course accepted immediately. I had a hunch that this could be my big journalism break, comparable to the time during the Watergate scandal when, in a secret meeting in a parking garage, the man known only as "Deep Throat" changed the course of history by giving Bob Woodward a really good water gun.

But not as good as the one that John Young sent me. This is not some flimsy plastic toy; this is a major contraption that weighs, when fully loaded, as much as a major kitchen appliance. It consists of a pressurized, water-filled fire-extinguisher tank that you wear in a harness on your back; this is connected via a short tube to a garden-hose nozzle riveted to the top of a gold motorcycle helmet, which you wear on your head, so that, when you squeeze a hand-held trigger, the water squirts out in whatever direction your head is pointing. You also wear a firefighter-style jacket that has been spray-painted silver; the jacket does not make the gun work any better, but it does perform the important function, in conjunction with the nozzle-topped helmet, of making you look like: Captain Bill, Space Dork!

I tested this water gun with my son, Rob, at a Miami gas station (we needed the station's air compressor to pressurize the tank). It is not easy, using mere words, to describe the feeling of power you get when, merely by squeezing your hand, you send a powerful jet of water whooshing from the top of your head, shooting 75 feet or more in whatever direction you look, but I will try: It is cool.

It also commands respect. At one point, two young men pulled up in a classic Bad Dude car—low to the ground, windows tinted with what appeared to be roofing tar, sound system thumping out bass notes loud enough to affect the

Earth's rotation. They stopped and got out, apparently intending to use the air compressor; but just then, Rob came around the front of my car, silver-coated, gold-helmeted, shooting a blast of water *over the gas-station roof*. The Bad Dudes were clearly startled, although they recovered and tried to look extremely unimpressed, as if to say, "Ho-hum, another Human Fire Hydrant." Then they got coolly, but quickly, back into their boombox car and thumped on out of there.

So we're talking about a powerful new technology here, and I've been pondering how it can best be utilized to benefit humanity in general, and I think I've figured out the ultimate use for the Ultimate Water Gun: Cigar Control.

As you know, cigars are now the "in" thing, with hip, fashionable, "with-it" sophisticates lighting up in restaurants and bars, apparently not realizing that, to the many, many people who don't care for cigars, it smells as though somebody has set an armpit on fire. (I am referring here to your cheaper cigar. Your more expensive cigar smells as though somebody has set a more expensive armpit on fire.)

Of course polite cigar smokers (and there are many) refrain from lighting up where others will unwillingly smell their smoke. But there seems to be a growing group of people—let's reach deep into our bag of euphemisms and call them "jerks"—who seem to *enjoy* lighting up in public places, who talk loudly and proudly about their cigars, as if they truly believe that the rest of us are *impressed* with a person capable of emitting this level of stench.

So picture this: You're in a restaurant, and a jerk lights up, and suddenly all the food tastes like cigar. You're wishing that somebody (not you; you don't want any trouble) would tell this guy exactly what he can do with his cigar; just then

WHAM the door bursts open, and there he is, his silver coat reflecting the candlelight—the Cigar Avenger! His gold helmet turns slowly, scanning the room, and suddenly he squeezes his hand trigger and *WHOOOSSH* the jerk is drenched from head to foot, with what looks like a wad of dead seaweed hanging limply from his clenched mouth.

As the surrounding diners break into applause, the jerk (he might be a lawyer) sputters: "THIS RESTAURANT HAS NO POLICY AGAINST CIGAR SMOKING!" And the Cigar Avenger calmly replies: "This restaurant also has no policy against extinguishing cigars with a powerful stream of water from a helmet-mounted spray nozzle."

And then, in a twinkle of silver, he is gone. Probably he is gone to get a hernia operation, because that thing is *heavy*.

THE INCREDIBLE SHRINKING BRAIN

I am feeling great, and I will tell you why. It's because of this article I read recently that said . . . um . . . it said . . . okay, wait just a minute while I get out this article . . .

Okay, here it is: According to this article, researchers at the University of Pennsylvania did a study showing that as males—but NOT females—get older, their brains shrink. Was I ever relieved to read that! I thought it was just me!

Here's something I regularly do: I'm walking through an airport, and I see a newsstand, and I think: "Huh! A newsstand! I can get a newspaper there, and perhaps some magazines! I can read them on the airplane, and use the information in them to write informed columns!"

So I carefully select some newspapers and magazines; then I put them on the counter; then I get out my wallet and pay for them; then I carefully put the receipt into my wallet so that I can deduct this purchase for tax purposes; then I go get on the airplane.

Okay, here's a pop quiz: What will I discover when I get on the airplane? You older, shrinking-brain males probably have no idea. You're saying to yourselves: "*What* airplane?"

But you female readers, and you younger males, know the answer: I will discover that I left my magazines and newspapers back on the newsstand counter. I cannot tell you how many times I have done this. (Note to Internal Revenue Service: The reason I still deduct these purchases on my tax return is that I am writing about them here.) I could save time if, when striding through the airport, I simply flung money in the general direction of the newsstand.

Here's another thing I do: I routinely go to the cleaners for the specific purpose of picking up my shirts, pay for my shirts, then attempt to walk out without my shirts, as though I were just visiting them.

Also: Many times I am looking *all over* for my reading glasses—looking, looking, looking, looking—and then I walk past a mirror and notice that they are perched on my head. "Ha ha!" they gaily shout to me, their lenses twinkling. "You cretin!"

Also: I have always been terrible at remembering people's names, but now I forget names *instantaneously*, before they have gotten all the way through my ear canal. If somebody introduces himself to me at a social event, it sounds as though he's saying: "Hi. I'm Blah."

"I'm sorry," I'll say. "What was your name again?"

"Blah," he'll say.

"Ah!" I'll say, smiling brightly while hoping that a meteor will crash into the building before I have to introduce him to someone else.

Here's another symptom: I currently own four—that is correct: four—identical, unused tubes of toothpaste, because every time I'm in a drugstore and walk past the toothpaste section, my brain, which by now must be about the size of a Raisinet, racks its tiny shriveled self in an effort to remember whether I have any toothpaste, and it can never come up with a definitive answer, so it always decides: Better safe than sorry!

(The good news is, if the price of Tartar Control Crest rises significantly, I will be a wealthy man.)

Anyway, I was very relieved to find out that this was not just my personal problem, but a problem afflicting the brains of males in general, although, as a frequent flier, I hope it doesn't extend to male airplane pilots ("Ladies and gentlemen, we are approaching either Pittsburgh or Honolulu, so at this time I'm going to push the button that either illuminates the fasten-seat-belt signs or shuts off all the engines").

The University of Pennsylvania study (Note to older males: I am referring here to a study showing that, as males get older, their brains shrink) also showed that we older males tend to lose our sense of humor. This is definitely true in my case. I was just talking to my oldest friend, whose name is . . . Excuse me while I look up his name . . . Okay, here it is: I was talking to my oldest friend, Joe DiGiacinto, and we were remarking on the fact that when we were teenage males roaming uncontrolled around Armonk, New York, we thought that the most hilarious imaginable human activity was the wanton destruction of mailboxes; whereas we now both firmly believe that this should be a federal crime punishable by death.

So my overall point is that the brain-shrinkage study makes me feel a lot better, because now I know that I'm not getting stupid alone; that billions of guys are getting stupid with me, as evidenced by:

- *Golf*
- *Comb-overs*

- *The U.S. Senate*
- *Marlon Brando*

Here's what I think: I think Older Male Brain Shrinkage (OMBS) should be recognized as a disability by the federal government. At the very least, we should have a law requiring everybody to wear a name tag ("HELLO! MY NAME IS BLAH"). Older males would be exempt from this requirement, because they wouldn't be able to find their tags. I have many other strong views on this subject, but I can't remember what they are.

ROAD WARRIORS

I got to thinking about courtesy the other day when a woman hit me with her car.

I want to stress that this was totally my fault. I was crossing a street in Miami, in a pedestrian crosswalk, and I saw the woman's car approaching, and like a total idiot I assumed she would stop. The reason I assumed this—you are going to laugh and laugh—is that there was a stop sign facing her, saying (this is a verbatim quote) "STOP."

I don't know what I was thinking. In Miami it is not customary to stop for stop signs. The thinking in Miami is, if you stop for a stop sign, the other motorists will assume that you are a tourist and therefore unarmed, and they will help themselves to your money and medically valuable organs. For the same reason, Miami drivers do not interpret traffic lights the same way as normal humans do. This is what a traffic light means to a Miami driver:

GREEN: Proceed
YELLOW: Proceed Much Faster
RED: Proceed While Gesturing

So anyway, there I was, Mr. Stupid Head, expecting a

Miami motorist to stop for a stop sign, and the result was that she had to slam on her brakes, and I had to leap backward like a character in a rental movie on rewind, and her car banged into my left knee.

I was shaken, but fortunately I remained calm enough to remember what leading medical authorities advise you to do if you are involved in an accident.

"Punch the car," they advise.

So I did. I punched the car, and I pointed to the stop sign, and, by way of amplification, I yelled "THERE'S A STOP SIGN!"

The woman then rolled down her window and expressed her deep remorse as follows: "DON'T HIT MY (UNLADY-LIKE WORD) CAR, YOU (VERY UNLADYLIKE WORD)!"

I should have yelled a snappy comeback, such as: "OH YEAH? WELL NOW, IN ADDITION TO MY KNEE, MY HAND HURTS!"

But before I could think of anything, she was roaring away, no doubt hoping to get through the next intersection while the light was still red.

The thing is, at the time I didn't think this incident was in any way remarkable. I had no doubt that people all over America were shouting bad words and coming to blows with each other's cars. It wasn't until two days later that I began thinking that maybe we could all be a little more courteous. What got me thinking this was England. I went there to attend a wedding in a scenic area called Gloucester-shire (pronounced "Wooster") near a lovely little town called Chipping Campden (tourism motto: "We've Got Your Sheep").

I'm not saying that the English are perfect. Their electrical fixtures look and function like science-fair projects; their plumbing apparently was designed thousands of years before the discovery of water. Also their television programming is not so great. The TV in my room got four channels, and one afternoon the program lineup, I swear, was:

- *Channel 1: A man talking about problems in the British gelatin industry;*
- *Channel 2: The national championships of an extremely slow-moving game called "snooker" (pronounced "Wooster");*
- *Channel 3: Another man (or possibly the same man) talking about problems in the British gelatin industry; and*
- *Channel 4: A show (this is the one I ended up watching) in which five people were taste-testing various brands of canned beef gravy and ranking them on a scale of 0 through 10.*

(Of course we have bad TV shows, too. But thanks to cable, we have infinitely more of them.) My point is that the English aren't better than us in every way. But they are definitely more courteous. It seems as though every time an English person comes even remotely close to being an inconvenience to anybody, he or she says "Sorry!" Often this causes the other person to say "Sorry!" for having been in a position to cause the first person to say "Sorry!" This may trigger reflex cries of "Sorry!" from random passersby, thereby setting off the legendary Chain Reaction of Sorrys, which sometimes does not stop until it reaches Wales.

I'm pretty sure that the Queen, when she's knighting somebody, taps him with her sword and says: "Sorry!"

Wouldn't it be nice if we had more of that spirit here? Wouldn't it be pleasant if we tried a little courtesy, instead of shooting each other over trivial provocations? Wouldn't it be wonderful if, when we irritated each other, we said "Sorry!" and *then* shot each other? At least it would be a start!

In fact, I'm going to start right here and now. I'm going to address the end of my column to the woman who hit me with her car, in case she's reading this:

Whoever you are, I am sincerely sorry that I impeded your progress through the stop sign. And I am even MORE sorry that I hit your car with my fist.

It should have been a hammer.

ABSOLUTE MADNESS

What I want to know is: Why is it important to have visible stomach muscles?

I grew up in an era (the Paleolithic) when people kept their stomach muscles discreetly out of sight. Most of us didn't even realize we *had* stomach muscles; the only people who ever actually saw them were courageous surgeons willing to cut through fat layers the thickness of the Cleveland white pages.

I'm not saying we weren't in shape; I'm just saying we had a different concept of what the shape should be. For example, our idea of a stud-muffin prototype male was somebody along the lines of George Reeves, who starred in the black-and-white TV version of *Superman,* playing the role of the mild-mannered newspaper reporter Clark Kent, whom nobody ever suspected of being Superman because he disguised himself by wearing glasses. (It is a known fact that if you put on glasses, even your closest friends will not recognize you; that's why, despite all the eerie similarities, nobody has ever figured out that Sally Jessy Raphael and Mike Tyson are actually the same person.)

The TV Superman, who was more powerful than a locomotive, did not have visible stomach muscles. In fact, he didn't have much muscle definition at all; he pretty much looked like a middle-aged guy at a Halloween party wearing a Superman costume made from pajamas, a guy who had definitely put in some time around the onion dip. From certain angles he looked as though he *weighed* more than a locomotive. But he got the job done. He was always flying to crime scenes faster than a speeding bullet in a horizontal position with his arms out in front of him.

Study Question: *Did he fly in this position because he HAD to? Or was it that the public would have been less impressed if he had flown in a sitting position, like an airline passenger, reading a magazine and eating honey-roasted peanuts?*

When Superman arrived at the crime scene, he would knock down the door, played by a piece of balsa wood, and confront the criminals, who were usually suit-wearing men with harsh voices. (You had a better-dressed criminal in those days.)

"Superman!" the criminals would say. This was the signal for Superman to put his hands on his hips so the criminals could shoot their revolvers at his chest, an effort that always caused Superman to adopt a bemused expression because, as a native of Krypton with special powers, he knew that the criminals were shooting blanks. Then Superman would turn the criminals over to the police, played by Irish character actors in their mid-sixties, after which he would fly in a horizontal position back to his secret Fortress of Onion Dip.

The point is that, in my era, Superman did not have visible stomach muscles, and neither did Hercules or Tarzan, who needed steel-reinforced vines. But now, suddenly, everybody is supposed to have rippling abdominals. They are hot. If muscle groups were rock bands, the abdominals would be Hootie & the Blowfish. Turn on your television, and if you do not see a commercial in which a leading economist such as Candice Bergen, Michael Jordan, or Whoopi Goldberg explains which long-distance carrier is best for your individual case (Answer: Whichever one is paying millions of dollars to Candice, Michael, or Whoopi), you will see the Abdominals People—and I do not wish to generalize here, but these people display the intelligence of sherbet—selling abdominal devices, demonstrating abdominal exercises, and of course proudly showing off their abdominal muscles, which bulge and writhe beneath a thin sweaty layer of skin, so that the people look as though they're smuggling pythons down there.

What I want to know is, why is this considered attractive? And how important, really, are abdominal muscles? I mean, I'm sure they serve some medical function, such as keeping your intestines from falling into your lap, but do they have to be HUGE? Do these people who spend seventeen hours a day building up their abdominals ever actually use them for any practical purpose? If so, what? Moving furniture? ("Okay, Thad, you push your awesome stomach muscles against THAT end of the bureau, and I'll push mine against THIS end, and we'll just . . . Huh! It's not moving!")

What I also want to know is: What's next? I mean, when the Abdominals People—formerly the Biceps People; formerly the Thighs People; formerly the Buns People—have made all the money they can from our stomachs, where will they go? Are they going to work their way through ALL of our muscles? Will there come a time, say ten years from now, when they're going to announce that we all need to build up, say, our eyelid muscles? Will we turn on the TV and see commercials for the Lid-A-Cizer, featuring enthusiastic men and women with form-fitting workout outfits and bulging eyelids the size of golf balls? Are we going to fall for THAT, too? Or are we going to draw the line somewhere? Think about it!

And while you're thinking, pass the dip.

Here are some members of a literary rock band called the Rock Bottom Remainders: *(from left)* Stephen King, Al Kooper, Ridley Pearson, me, and Tad Bartimus. We sound almost as good as we look.

PLANET OF THE APES

You don't realize it, but you are constantly enjoying the benefits of science. For example, when you turn on the radio, you take it for granted that music will come out; but do you ever stop to think that this miracle would not be possible without the work of scientists? That's right: There are tiny scientists inside that radio, playing instruments! A similar principle is used in automatic bank-teller machines, which is why they frequently say: "SORRY, OUT OF SERVICE." They're too embarrassed to say: "SORRY, TINY SCIENTIST GOING TO THE BATHROOM."

Yes, science plays a vital role in your life; but when it comes to scientific knowledge, there's an excellent chance that you're a moron. I base this statement on a recent survey, conducted by the National Science Foundation, which showed that the average American does not understand basic scientific principles. Naturally the news media reported this finding as though it were shocking, which is silly. This is, after all, a nation that has produced tournament bass fishing *and* the Home Shopping Channel; we should be shocked that the average American still knows how to walk erect.

But the point is that we have a scientific illiteracy problem in this nation, and you could be a part of it. To find out, see if you can answer these three actual questions from the National Science Foundation survey:

1. True or False: The earliest human beings lived at the same time as the dinosaurs.
2. Which travels faster, light or sound?
3. Explain, in your own words: What is DNA?

All finished? Now let's look at the correct answers:

1. FALSE. The truth is that the dinosaurs had been dead for over a week before the first human came along, probably in the form of Bob Dole. Yet most Americans firmly believe that humans and dinosaurs once coexisted. This misconception arose from the many absurdly inaccurate fictional depictions of caveman life, such as the TV cartoon show *The Flintstones,* in which the Flintstones own a pet dinosaur named Dino. But paleontologists, who can determine the age of fossils with a high degree of accuracy using a technique called "carbon dating," have known for many years that "Dino" is actually another character wearing a costume. "We think it's Barney," the paleontologists announced recently, "but we can't say for sure until we get another government grant."

2. To answer the light-vs.-sound question, consider what you observe when a thunderstorm is approaching and a bolt of lightning strikes. First you see the lightning bolt; then you hear thunder; then you hear a scream if the lightning bolt has struck a person; then you hear a loud cheer from bystanders if the person was George Steinbrenner. This tells us that light travels faster than sound, because

light goes straight down from the sky and is therefore attracted by gravity; whereas sound goes sideways and is slowed down by friction with the Earth's rotation, also known as "peristalsis," or "The Greenhouse Effect."

3. "DNA" is an abbreviation for "deoxyribonucleicantidisestablishmentarianism," a complex string of syllables that is found inside your body in tiny little genes called "chromosomes." Biologists often refer to DNA as "The Body's Secret Handshake," because the information encoded in your DNA determines your unique biological characteristics, such as sex, eye color, age, and Social Security number.

There is surprisingly little difference between the DNA found in humans and that found in other species such as H. Ross Perot. This fact has led to research that could benefit mankind, most notably a series of experiments in which biologists chemically altered the DNA in fruit flies in an effort to isolate the gene that causes baldness. The biologists reasoned that fruit flies must contain this gene, because virtually all of them (the fruit flies) (also the biologists) are bald. This work took nine years and cost $31 million, but the results were impressive: When a group of fruit flies with normal DNA were compared with a group with altered DNA, both groups were found to consist of little random black smears, because the only way the biologists could get them to hold still was to whack them with rolled-up copies of *Scientific American*. Nevertheless the biologists believe that they are on the right track.

"We think it's Barney wearing a Dino costume," they announced recently in a press conference that led to allegations of plagiarism from angry paleontologists, "but we can't say for sure until we get another government grant."

So those are your correct answers. If you did poorly, you're not alone; the National Science Foundation reports that only 25 percent of the people surveyed, or 1 in 6, passed the quiz. And if you think that's a pathetic commentary on our national intelligence, you should see all the mail I'm going to get in which people will send me this column with the words "25 percent" and "1 in 6" circled and a snotty note informing me that this is incorrect.

So there's no question about it: Scientific illiteracy is definitely a major problem in America. And as the saying goes: "If you're not part of the solution, you're a newspaper columnist." So I feel I've done my part. And now, if you'll excuse me, I have to shake the radio.

GOOD FOR WHAT AILS YOU

W e here at the Bureau of Medical Alarm hope you had a restful, carefree, fun-filled summer. But before you get back into "the swing of things" for fall, we'd like to take just a moment to remind you that practically everything can kill you.

Latex Gloves of Death

We have here a Health Advisory issued June 27 by the U.S. Food and Drug Administration (motto: "We Have Not Yet Determined That Our Motto Is Safe"). This advisory, which was sent in by several alert medical people, begins with the following statement:

"In the spring and summer of 1995, the spontaneous combustion of powder-free latex patient examination gloves caused four fires in different states."

The advisory states that all four fires involved large quantities of gloves stored in hot warehouses. But we here at the Bureau of Medical Alarm are asking ourselves: What if a single glove (this is sometimes called the "Lone Glove" theory) were to burst into flames? What if this happened while the glove was on a doctor's hand? And what if the doctor's hand was, at that very moment, *inside your personal body?*

One thing that would happen, of course, is the doctor would charge you a lot of money. The underlying philosophy of our entire health-care system is that the more scary, painful, dangerous, and unnecessary a medical procedure is, the more it should cost. So you would definitely pay top dollar to have a flaming glove thrust into what is technically known as the Booty Region. Once word of this lucrative new procedure got around, doctors would be prescribing it for athlete's foot.

And here's a related item to be concerned about: An alert dental surgeon named Ian Hamilton sent me the June 1996 newsletter of the Canterbury Branch of the New Zealand Dental Association, which contains a letter to the editor, accompanied by a photograph, concerning a latex medical glove that was found to have a *moth* embedded in one of the fingers. Yes. This means you could wind up with a *burning rubberized insect* inside your body. Imagine the bill you'd get for THAT:

Flaming Booty Moth Treatment (FBMT)—$578,000
Recharge Fire Extinguisher—$23
Damage to Doctor's Golf Grip—$54,000,000,000

We know what you're wondering at this point. You're wondering: "Wouldn't 'The Flaming Booty Moths' be a great name for a rock band?"

Yes, it would. But right now you have other important medical things to worry about, such as:

Deadly Items Up Your Nose

We have here a news item from the *Denver Post,* written by Jim Kirksey and sent in by many alert readers, concerning a man who arrived at a hospital "with a device in his sinus cavity that potentially had the explosive force of five powerful M-80 firecrackers." The device was a trigger used to deploy automobile air bags; the man worked at a factory that manufactures the triggers, and an explosion had caused one of them to become—in the words of a surgeon—"lodged into his nose."

Fortunately, the device was safely removed, but the doctors were very nervous that it might go off during the surgery. Here at the Bureau of Medical Alarm we are wondering: Why doesn't the federal government require auto manufacturers to warn us that air bags contain devices that could be deadly if we get them up our noses? This is especially critical if we have very young children, who can get ANYTHING up their noses. Very young children can get things up their noses that are larger than their BODIES. We think the government should require that the following statement be printed on automobile steering wheels:

WARNING—DO NOT ALLOW VERY YOUNG CHILDREN TO DISASSEMBLE THE AIR BAG AND INSERT THE EXPLOSIVE TRIGGER DEVICE WAY UP THEIR NOSES, AS THIS COULD RESULT IN YOUR HAVING TO SPEND THE REST OF YOUR MORTAL LIFE TRYING TO EXPLAIN THINGS TO YOUR INSURANCE

COMPANY. ALSO, YOU SHOULD NOT ATTEMPT TO READ THIS WARNING WHILE OPERATING THIS . . . LOOK OUT!! (CRASH) TOO LATE.

On a related medical note, we received a letter from Gail White, who works at a large hospital that shall remain nameless, and who relates the following incident:

"A man appeared at the emergency room with his hands over his face, demanding to see a MALE doctor, and to see him ALONE. A doctor (dreading to see some horrible disfigurement) complied with his wishes. When the man removed his hands, he was revealed to have a brassiere caught in his nose by the hooks."

No, we do not know how the brassiere got caught there. Nor do we know how many men are, right now, suffering from Brassiere Nose, but are too embarrassed to seek medical treatment. Our best guess is: thousands. If you are one of these unfortunate people, we urge you to seek medical help; your doctor can tell you about a revolutionary new procedure to correct this condition. Tell him you definitely want the moth.

EUREKA!

People often ask me how America became the world's greatest economic power, as measured in Remote Control Units Per Household (RCUPH).

My answer is: "Inventions."

Americans have always been great inventors. To cite one historic example: Back in 1879, a young man named Thomas Alva Edison was trying to develop a new light source. One day he was messing around in his laboratory with some filaments when suddenly a thought struck him: The letters in "Thomas Alva Edison" could be rearranged to spell "Do Have Salami Snot." This made him so depressed that he invented the phonograph, so he could listen to B.B. King records.

A more recent example of American inventiveness is "Buffalo-style" chicken wings. For many years, nobody ate chicken wings, and for a good reason: They are inedible. They are essentially meat-free bones. You might as well chew on a plate of toenails. But one day a shrewd restaurant owner came up with the idea of serving the wings "Buffalo-style," which means "to people who have been drinking beer." It is a known fact that beer-drinkers will eat pretty much anything: Exhibit A is "Slim Jims." You could put a dish of salted mothballs in front of beer-drinkers, and they would snork them up. So chicken wings were an instant hit.

Today, "Buffalo-style" chicken wings are served in restaurants all over the nation: The waitperson brings out a plate of bones, the customers gnaw on them for a while, and then the waitperson takes them back to the kitchen, where they're run through the dishwasher and placed on a plate for the next set of customers to gnaw on. A restaurant can sell the same set of "Buffalo-style" wings hundreds of times; this provides a big boost to the economy, and it is easier on the chickens.

And speaking of modern inventions, let's talk about the incredible convenience of cellular phones, especially for motorists. Years ago, when you were driving, you wasted your time on such nonproductive activities as listening to the radio, steering, etc. But now, using your cellular phone, you can engage in productive conversations ("Hello, Ted? Can you hear me? Hello? Ted? Can you . . . Hello? Ted? Can . . . Hello?"). As a safety bonus, you can also use your cellular phone to call for an ambulance after you rear-end somebody ("Hello? 911? Can you hear . . . Hello?").

The exciting thing is, at this very moment, Americans are thinking up inventions that could improve our lifestyles *even more*. For example, a while back I received a letter from a research scientist (unfortunately, I lost the letter, so I can't give you his name) who told me that he and some other research scientists were working on developing a system for—I believe this is how he worded it—"transmitting frozen margaritas over ordinary telephone lines." I speak for Americans everywhere when I say: Let's track these scientists down and give them a large federal grant.

I received another letter, which I managed not to lose,

from alert reader Dick Demers, who told me about some inventions that he and his friends had conceived of. For example, his friend James Cathey thought up the long-overdue idea of a "briefcase aquarium." I assume this would be an aquarium that had a handle so you could carry it around with you; thus, if you were stuck in, for example, a company meeting wherein your boss was droning away about improving product quality, you could pass the time productively by watching your fish swim around and poop.

Another one of Demers's friends, Richard Jeanne, had a fine idea for improving the quality of motoring experience. You know those irritating drivers who leave their turn signals blinking, sometimes all the way from New York to Cleveland, slowly driving you insane? This irritation would be eliminated by Jeanne's idea for a new, improved turn signal: "After 15 seconds, the car will automatically turn in the direction indicated by the signal." Wouldn't that be great? It would remove at least 200,000 drivers from the road in Miami alone. Speaking of irritations: Have you noticed that more people seem to be paying for everything—EVERYTHING—with credit cards? Last winter I waited in a long ticket line outside a movie theater near Detroit on a bitterly cold night for what seemed like hours because many people were charging their $3.50 movie tickets. Each of these purchases had to be approved by a central computer; meanwhile, the movie was starting, and people in the ticket line were keeling over from frostbite and being dragged off into the parking lot by wolves. I have invented a way to prevent this kind of thing: For credit-card purchases under $20, the central computer would add an Annoyance Charge, which would be based on the number of people waiting in line, air temperature, and other factors. ("Okay, that's two tickets to *Flipper;* with your senior-citizen discount and your Annoyance Charge, it comes to $237,000.")

I'll bet you have some good invention ideas, too, and I'd love to hear what they are. But please mail them in; we cannot accept phone calls. We're keeping the line open for margaritas.

BEEWARE

Today's Science Topic Is: Insect Intelligence

I don't know about you, but I've always taken comfort in the idea that insects are stupid. For example, if I'm outdoors and a bee lands on me and starts walking around on my head—causing me to turn rigid with fear, terrified that, if I move, the bee will become angry and sting me in the eyeball—I've always reassured myself by thinking: "This bee does not wish to harm me! Its tiny brain is confused! It thinks I am a flower!"

But now I have received, from alert reader Greg Stevens, a news item by the Reuters (pronounced "Associated Press") news service concerning an experiment, conducted by bee scientists at the Free University of Berlin, suggesting that bees are not so dumb after all.

The article states that these scientists, whose names are "Lars" and "Karl," set up various landmarks between a beehive and a bee feeder. After the bees had located the feeder, Lars and Karl started changing the locations of the feeder and landmarks. The surprising result: Lars and Karl were both killed by eyeball stings.

No, seriously, they discovered that the bees were locating the feeder by *counting the landmarks*. Yes! Bees can count! This means that bees, in terms of math skills, are ahead of most American high school graduates. It also means that, contrary to my earlier belief, when a bee is walking around on my head, it knows exactly where it is and what it's doing. It's thinking: "Ha ha! He thinks I'm looking for a flower, when in fact I am here for the express written purpose of watching him turn rigid with terror while I poop in his hair! I can't wait to get back to the hive and tell everybody the landmark coordinates for THIS bozo!"

The German discovery makes you wonder what ELSE bees have been hiding from us. For example: I have always wondered how they *really* obtain honey. I do not believe that they make it themselves. What would they use for utensils? I've never made honey, but I have made fudge, which belongs to the same chemical family (technically, the "Family of Things You Can Put on Ice Cream"), and I know for a fact that you need, at minimum, a stove and a candy thermometer. My guess is, if you were to poke around in the bushes near a beehive, you'd find piles of empty plastic squeeze bottles shaped like little bears.

But here's what really concerns me: If bees can count, the logical assumption is that they can also read. Therefore, I wish to make a sincere announcement to any bees walking around on this newspaper: I DID NOT BLOW UP THE HIVE NEAR EVAN THOMPSON'S HOUSE IN ARMONK, NEW YORK, IN 1961. I WAS PRESENT, BUT IT WAS EVAN WHO LIT THE CHERRY BOMB. PLEASE DO NOT HURT ME. IT IS VERY FUNNY WHEN YOU POOP IN MY HAIR. HA HA! I BELIEVE EVAN STILL LIVES IN THE NEW YORK METROPOLITAN AREA. THANK YOU.

Here is another troubling thought: Bees are not the only smart insects. I have here an item from the November 1995 issue of *Popular Science,* alertly sent in by Frank Schropfer, which states that cockroaches can display intelligent behavior *even when their heads have been removed.* I don't know about you, but I didn't even know cockroaches *had* heads. I thought that, as members of what biologists call the "Family of Animals That It Is Morally Okay to Drop an Unabridged Dictionary On," cockroaches were just icky little brown bodies with legs and feelers sticking out. But it turns out that they do have heads, and according to *Popular Science,* they "can live for several days" without them. But here's the amazing thing: Researchers have found that cockroaches, when their heads are removed, immediately start performing country-style line dances.

No, seriously, *Popular Science* states that headless cockroaches can, when prompted by electrical shocks, *learn to run a maze.* Without heads! They can learn a maze *in thirty minutes.* I seriously doubt that headless humans could beat that time, although just to be sure we should definitely run some experiments using volunteer Tobacco Institute scientists.

I also think we should find out what, exactly, the researchers do with the cockroach heads. You would definitely want heavy security for those babies. You would NOT want them to fall into the wrong hands.

> *Tom Brokaw: In our top story tonight, terrorists have threatened that, unless the United States government gives them Cincinnati, they are going to dump cockroach heads into the nation's vulnerable supply of movie popcorn. For the Clinton administration's reaction, we go now live to*

White House press secretary Mike McCurry, who has a statement.

McCurry: *I'm going to throw up.*

In conclusion, we see that the issue of insect intelligence is not as simple as we thought it was before we started to think about it. So the next time a mosquito lands on our arm, and we are tempted to whack it, we should pause and remind ourselves that the mosquito is a thinking being just like us; and that, with proper training and encouragement, it might be able not only to count and run mazes, but perhaps also to laugh, to sing, to philosophize, even to write poetry.

And then we should whack it. Because we hate poetry.

THE NEW MAD SCIENCE

Today I wish to present further evidence that the scientific community has completely lost its mind.

Exhibit A is an article that appeared recently on the front page of the *New York Times* (motto: "Even We Don't Read the Whole Thing"). The article concerns a scientist named Dr. Raul J. Cano, who got hold of a bee that died 30 million years ago and was preserved in amber.

Now here is the difference between a scientist and a sane layperson such as yourself: If YOU came across a bee that had been dead for 30 million years, your natural, common-sense reaction would be to stomp on it just in case, then maybe use it as part of a prank involving a salad bar. But that was not Dr. Cano's scientific reaction. His reaction—and remember, this story comes from the *New York Times*, which never makes anything up—was to extract some really old dead germs from the bee's stomach AND BRING THEM BACK TO LIFE.

Yes. Does this make ANY sense to you? I mean, don't we already have ENOUGH live germs in this world, causing disease, B.O., and really implausible movies starring Dustin

Hoffman? Do we laypersons not spend billions of dollars per year on antibiotics, Listerine, Right Guard, and Ty-D-Bol for the specific purpose of KILLING germs?

According to the *Times*, the scientific community is all excited about Dr. Cano's revived bee-stomach germs. Apparently the scientific community has never seen *The Mummy, Frankenstein, Night of the Living Dead, Bacteria,* or any of the numerous other reputable motion pictures depicting the bad things that inevitably happen when some fool brings a dead organism back to life. You wait: One of these nights, Dr. Cano's germs are going to escape from their petri dishes and start creeping forward, zombie-like, with their little bacterial arms sticking straight out in front of them, and heaven help the laboratory security guard who stands in their way. ("What's wrong, Bob?" "I don't know! I have the weirdest feeling something's trying to eat my toe!")

At this point you are saying, "Okay, so this one scientist is perhaps a few ice cubes short of a tray. But he's probably just an isolated example."

You wish. I have here another *New York Times* story, sent in by many alert readers, concerning scientists who have figured out how to—get ready—GROW EXTRA EYES ON FLIES. Yes. The story states that, by messing around with genes, the scientists have produced flies with "as many as fourteen eyes apiece" in various locations—"on their wings, on their legs, on the tips of their antennae."

On behalf of normal humans everywhere, let me just say: Great! Just what we need! Flies that can see EVEN BETTER! As I write these words, I am unwillingly sharing my lunch with a regular, nonimproved fly, which is having no trouble whatsoever seeing well enough to keep an eye on me while it walks around on my peanut-butter sandwich. Whenever

I try to whap it, the fly instantly zooms out of reach, buzzing its wings to communicate, in fly language, the concept of "neener neener."

Not that it would do me any good to kill it; Dr. Raul J. Cano would probably just bring it back to life.

Speaking of insects, I have here a column from the spring 1995 issue of *American Entomologist* magazine, sent in by alert reader Jackie Simons and written by May Berenbaum, who discusses a University of Illinois entomology professor who has—you are not going to believe this, but I'm going to tell you anyway—"pioneered the design and use of artificial limbs for cockroaches."

Naturally I had to call this professor, whose name is Fred Delcomyn. He freely admitted to me that he has, indeed, fitted cockroaches with tiny artificial limbs made from toothpicks. He's trying to figure out exactly how cockroaches move—in stark contrast to us normal, nonscientist, sane people, who would like to figure out exactly how to make cockroaches STOP moving, so we could hit them with hammers.

But here's the truly alarming thing: Delcomyn, as part of his research, wants to BUILD A ROBOT COCKROACH. In fact, he has already built one that's a foot and a half long ("not too big, compared to your Florida roaches," he noted, correctly). But his plan is to build a bigger one, a robot cockroach that will be FOUR FEET LONG.

When will these scientists ever learn? We know what's going to happen! We've seen this movie! Everything will be fine at first, with the robot roach doing exactly what the scientists want it to. But then one night, after the scientists have left the laboratory, there will be a lightning storm, and extra electricity will flow into the roach, and it will COME

TO LIFE ON ITS OWN—FrankenRoach!—and escape and terrorize the community, smashing its way into supermarkets, skittering past terrified screaming shoppers, seizing entire display racks of Hostess Twinkies.

Oh sure, eventually the Army will come up with a way to stop it, possibly by constructing a fifty-foot-tall can of Raid. But do we really want to put ourselves through this? Why must scientists continue to mess with the natural order of things? Why do we need to create giant cockroaches? We already have the O.J. Simpson defense team! If you are as concerned about these issues as I am, I urge you to take action TODAY in the form of doubling your medication dosage. Also, you are welcome to this sandwich.

MY SUMMER VACATION

Once again it's summer vacation time—time to lock up the house, load the kids into the car, fill the tank with gas, then decide which one of the kids you should sell to pay for the gas, because it's very expensive this year.

Now you're all set! To guarantee that it's the "vacation of a lifetime," I've prepared a special itinerary just for you, featuring a set of unique attractions that I swear I am not making up.

You'll start by driving to . . .

Marshall County, Indiana—Here you'll visit the historic town of Bremen. According to the Marshall County Convention and Tourism Commission brochure, sent to me by alert reader Chris Straight, Bremen's claim to fame is that "the world's heaviest man died here." The brochure offers no details, except to say that while in Bremen, you can "ask about the casket preparation for the world's heaviest man." It doesn't say whom, specifically, you should ask. Your best bet is to just drive into Bremen, honk at the first person you see, roll down your window, and shout: "WHAT ABOUT THE CASKET PREPARATION FOR THE

WORLD'S HEAVIEST MAN?" Then you should drum your fingers impatiently on the steering wheel to indicate you need a quick answer, because you're in a hurry to get to your next vacation destination. . . .

Macklin, Saskatchewan—This is located in Canada, which is legally a foreign country, but it's well worth the trip, because Macklin is the proud home of the world's largest fiberglass replica of the ankle bone of a horse. This particular one stands 32 feet high, which makes it taller than any fiberglass horse ankle bone you're going to see in your so-called sophisticated cities such as New York or Paris.

The giant ankle bone, which was brought to my attention by alert reader Marylu Walters, symbolizes a game called "bunnock" ("bones"), in which you try to knock over horse bones by throwing other horse bones at them. According to a brochure put out by the Macklin Bunnock Committee, the game was invented by Russian soldiers in Siberia who "discovered that the ankle bones of a horse could be set up on the frozen ground." The brochure, speculating on what inspired this discovery, suggests "ingenuity," "sheer luck," and "boredom," although I personally think that another strong candidate would be "vodka."

Your family is sure to enjoy viewing the giant Macklin bunnock, which looks vaguely like an enormous naked woman with no arms or legs or head. If you're lucky enough to be in Macklin in August, you might witness the World Championship Bunnock Tournament. But as much fun as it is to watch Canadians throw horse bones, you need to move on to . . .

Easton, Massachusetts—This, according to a *Boston Globe* article alertly sent in by Tom Darisse, is the home of the nation's only Shovel Museum. More than 800 shovels!

The kids will forget all about Disney World! But you'll have to pry them away, because you're off to . . .

Reno, Nevada—It was here, at the Reno-Sparks sewage treatment plant, where, on February 4, according to a lengthy article in the *Reno Gazette-Journal* sent in by many alert readers, two courageous plant workers used pitchforks to apprehend a "monster grease ball." The article states that the grease ball, which was clogging a channel leading to the plant, weighed 150 pounds and was "human-sized," which leads to the obvious question: Was Robert Shapiro reported missing at around that time?

Tragically, the grease ball is not on public display, but you and your family will be able to enjoy a quick picnic near the historic sewage plant before hastening to your final vacation destination. . . .

Fort Collins, Colorado—Why Fort Collins? I'll answer that question by quoting verbatim the first paragraph of a story from the February 22 *Fort Collins Coloradoan*, written by Dan Haley and alertly sent in by Glenn Gilbert:

"About 200 human gonads are sitting in a freezer at Colorado State University as researchers wait for funding to test them for plutonium."

I called Colorado State ("Home of the Frozen Gonads") and spoke with Dr. Shawki Ibrahim, an associate professor in the Department of Radiological Health Sciences. He told me that the gonads were removed during hospital autopsies; researchers want to find out if their plutonium levels correlate with how close their former owners lived to the Rocky Flats nuclear weapons plant. (The researchers need money for this project, so if you're a wealthy organization, please send them some.)

Dr. Ibrahim told me that the gonads are very valuable,

and are kept in a locked freezer in a secure area. "We are sitting on a gold mine here," he said. (Really.)

I definitely see the need for security. You cannot have unsecured gonads in an environment frequented by college students; the potential for pranks is too great. This means you will NOT be able to actually see anything during your visit to Fort Collins. You will, however, be able to say, "Kids, we're standing within a mile or so of about two hundred frozen human gonads!"

Trust me, it will be a vacation memory that will remain in their minds for the rest of their lives. Even after electroshock therapy.

MY SON THE TEENAGE DRIVER

My son is learning to drive. This terrifies me. He's four years old.

Well, okay, technically he's fifteen. But from the perspective of the aging parent, there is no major difference between four and fifteen, except that when your child is four, his motoring privileges are restricted to little toy Fisher-Price vehicles containing little toy Fisher-Price people who are unlikely (although I would not totally rule it out, in America) to sue you.

Whereas when your child turns fifteen, the state of Florida lets him obtain a permit that allows him to drive an actual car on actual roads, despite the fact that you can vividly remember when he slept on *Return of the Jedi* sheets. Of course there are restrictions: He must be accompanied by a licensed driver age eighteen or over. But that does not reassure me. What that means to me is that, in the eyes of the state of Florida, it is perfectly okay for my son to be driving around accompanied only by Ted Kennedy.

I want tougher restrictions than that. I want the law to say that if my son is going to drive, he must be accompanied by a licensed paramedic and at least two Supreme Court justices. Also I believe that, as a safety precaution, his car should be attached via a stout chain to a restraining device such as the Pentagon.

It's not that I think my son is a bad driver. He's actually a pretty *good* driver, careful to signal his turns. That's what worries me: He'll be driving in Miami, where nobody else, including the police, does this. If Miami motorists were to see a turn signal, there's no telling how they'd react. They could become alarmed and start shooting.

And what if my son actually believes the official Florida state driver's manual when it says that the left lane is for passing only? Not here in Miami, it isn't! The driving public here apparently believes that there is some kind of deadly voodoo curse on the right lane, so *everybody* drives in the left lane here, at speeds ranging all the way from Indianapolis 500 down to Car Wash. This means that if you get behind somebody traveling at, say, Funeral Procession, and you want to pass, you have to disregard the driver's manual, risk the voodoo curse, and use the right lane, UNLESS the driver in front of you is talking on a cellular telephone, because these people frequently receive urgent mandatory instructions from whoever they're talking to, such as "SWERVE ACROSS ALL AVAILABLE LANES IMMEDIATELY!" So when you're behind cell-phone drivers, it's generally wise to wait patiently for a few moments until they ram into a bridge abutment; then you can pass safely on whichever side has the least amount of flame spewing out.

We veteran Miami drivers know this, just as we know

that, in Miami, it's considered acceptable to park on any semi-level surface including roofs, and to go through a red light as long as you can still remember when it was yellow. But how is my son supposed to know these things?

What really scares me is, he'll want to drive a LOT. I know this, because I remember exactly how I felt when I got my driver's license, in 1963. I was a student at Pleasantville (New York) High School, where, if you were a male, cars were *extremely* important. There were two major religions: Ford and Chevy. Ford guys would carve "FoMoCo" (for "Ford Motor Company") on desks; Chevy guys—this was considered extremely witty—would change it to read "FoNoGo." We found great wisdom in Beach Boys car songs, which are just like love songs to a woman, except they're (a) more passionate, and (b) more technically detailed, as in these lyrics from "Little Deuce Coupe":

She's ported and relieved and she's stroked and bored;
She'll do a hundred and forty in the top end floored . . .

At lunchtime we stood next to the circle in front of the high school and watched guys drive around slowly, revving their engines. Sometimes, if we were especially impressed with a car, we would spit.

I applied for my New York state driver's license the instant I was old enough, and the day it arrived—finally!—in the mail, I borrowed my mother's car, which was a Plymouth Valiant station wagon that could attain a top speed of 53 miles per hour if dropped from a bomber. I didn't care: *I had wheels.* I drove around at random for approximately the next two years. It made no difference to me where I was going. I was happy simply to be in motion, with the AM radio turned up loud and tuned to WABC in New York City, which would be playing, say, "He's So Fine" by the Chiffons:

> He's so fine (Doo-lang doo-lang doo-lang)
> Wish he were mine (Doo-lang doo-lang doo-lang)
> That handsome boy over there . . .

And behind the wheel, with my arm draped casually out the window, I imagined that I WAS that handsome boy, not some dweeb driving his mom's Valiant. I was cool. I was *driving*.

These days when I'm driving I rarely listen to music. I do listen to traffic reports, because I'm always late for some obligatory grown-up thing. I'm never driving just to be driving.

But my son will be, soon. He'll be out there every chance he gets, feeling so fine, cruising to nowhere, signaling his turns, playing his music, cranking it up when a good song comes on, maybe exchanging high-fives with the Supreme Court justices.

Yup, he'll be on the road a lot—a teenager, but still, in many ways, a human being. Please watch out for him.

INVASION OF THE
KILLER LAWYERS

Could alien beings from another galaxy come here and obliterate human civilization? If so, would this be covered by our homeowners' insurance?

These troubling questions are on the minds of the millions of people who are being exposed this summer to the spectacle of grotesque, repulsive, inhuman creatures that would stop at nothing in their determination to dominate the Earth. I am referring, of course, to the Democratic and Republican conventions.

But the public was also troubled by the blockbuster motion picture *Independence Day*. It definitely had a powerful effect on me. I had been skeptical about all the "hype," but when the two-and-a-half-hour movie was over, I found myself sitting pensively in the theater for quite a while, pondering the question: How am I going to get out of here when my shoes are bonded in place by one of the most powerful adhesives known to science, Movie Floor Crud, which is a mixture of Pepsi, Milk Duds, and year-old nasal secretions snorted out by distraught moviegoers during the ending of *The Bridges of Madison County*? A lot of people just leave their shoes on the theater floor and walk out barefoot.

But getting back to *Independence Day*: What happens is, these aliens from millions of light-years away arrive in our solar system in a fantastically huge spaceship manufactured by the Winnebago Corporation. When they reach Earth, they are in a bad mood, possibly because their luggage has not arrived, so they attack New York City, causing the population to panic and run around screaming.

In my opinion, this is the only unrealistic part of the movie. I mean, we're talking about *New Yorkers*, here. These are tough people. These are people who, every day, without even thinking about it, voluntarily go down into dark, steaming, noisy, extremely aromatic holes containing the New York City subway system. People who do that are not going to get bent out of shape just because an alien invasion force is obliterating their city. They are merely going to shrug and continue reading the *New York Post* (front-page headline: *UFO ATTACK DESTROYS BUTTAFUOCO HOME*).

At the same time as they hit New York, the aliens destroy Los Angeles—a clear indication that they had been monitoring the O.J. Simpson trial. They also wipe out Washington, D.C., apparently believing—this just shows that even a highly advanced species can be stupid—that wiping out the federal government would somehow make it more difficult for the country to function.

While millions of Americans take to the streets to celebrate the fact that they will probably not have to file income-tax returns for several years, the president of the United States, played by a weenie, escapes, along with several key actors, to an ultra-secret government installation.

There they learn that scientists have been trying to repair an alien flying saucer that crashed in 1947, which means the warranty has expired. (This crash was hushed up, except for a brief statement from the Federal Aviation Administration assuring the public that flying-saucer travel is perfectly safe.) The secret installation also contains the bodies of deceased aliens, which have likewise been kept completely hidden away except for one brief incident in 1977 when one of them showed up as part of a science-fair project submitted by Amy Carter.

The plot thickens when Jeff Goldblum, who plays a brilliant cable-TV scientist, discovers, by analyzing signals coming from the extraterrestrial Mother Ship, that the aliens are the source of all "infomercials." This makes the Earth so mad that it decides to fight back. There is a spectacular aerial battle between a fleet of scale-model alien saucers and a fleet of scale-model Air Force fighters, led by President Weenie. Meanwhile, Jeff Goldblum, flying in the crashed enemy saucer, which is piloted by the Fresh Prince of Bel-Air, gets inside the mother ship and uses his laptop computer to put a virus into the aliens' main computer system. He can do this because the aliens, like every other life form in the galaxy, have basically no choice but to use the Windows 95 operating system; in fact the whole reason why they have attacked the Earth is to destroy Bill Gates.

Goldblum's virus easily disables the aliens' main computer. Perhaps you're wondering why aliens who can travel millions of light-years can't fix a computer virus. The answer is that, like any large organization, the Mother Ship has only one individual who actually understands the computer system, and that individual is not available. The alien computer nerd is hiding in the bowels of the Mother Ship, playing the alien version of Space Invaders, in which the object is to kill little attacking figures that look like Keanu Reeves.

So, the alien ships, their defenses disabled, are all shot down, and the movie ends with people all over the world celebrating. Of course the cheering will stop soon enough, when millions of attorneys crawl out of the smoking rubble of America's cities, contact the surviving aliens, put neck braces on them, and start suing the Earth in general for trillions of dollars. THAT'S when we should really get worried.

BOY GENIUS

To be honest, I had completely forgotten that in a former life I was Mozart. You know how certain things tend to slip your mind, like where you left your car keys, or the fact that you used to be a brilliant Austrian composer who died in 1791? Well, that's exactly what happened to me.

I was reminded of my former life recently when I received a book called *Spirit at Work*, by Lois Grant, who has had a number of former lives. (I realize that some of you may be skeptical about the idea of reincarnation, but there's a lot of evidence that it's real. Exhibit A is Vice President Al Gore, who obviously, at some point in his previous existence, was a slab of Formica.)

Besides having been reincarnated, Lois Grant is in close personal touch with many spiritual entities, including her deceased cat, Fluffernut, and the Archangel Michael, who has written a nice blurb for the cover of *Spirit at Work*, which he calls "a key to the rebirth of the planet." (I myself have never gotten a blurb quite that positive, although one of my books was described as being "heavy on the booger jokes," which is similar.)

Anyway, it turns out that one whole chapter of *Spirit at Work* is devoted to some correspondence that Lois Grant and I had back in 1991. It began when she wrote me a long letter, in which she said that she had been asking herself the question—I bet you've asked this question many times—"Where is Mozart now?" So she decided to contact Joya Pope, who serves as a "channeler" for a spiritual entity named Michael, who is "a group of 1,050 souls who have completed their cycle of lives on the Earth." (Sounds like the U.S. Congress!)

Through Joya—who according to the book "is available for channeling by telephone"—Lois Grant asked Michael about the current whereabouts of Mozart. The answer was: "He is a writer living in Florida." On a hunch, Lois Grant sent Joya a photograph of me from the newspaper, and the answer came back that the current reincarnation of Wolfgang Amadeus Mozart is none other than—you guessed it—Wayne Newton.

No, seriously, according to Lois Grant, Joya/Michael says that I used to be Mozart. I was quite surprised to learn this, and you would have been, too, if you had seen me take piano lessons. This was in 1956, when the piano teacher, a woman named Mrs. Ugly Old Bat, used to come to my house every Saturday on her broom and point out to my mother that I apparently had not been practicing.

This was of course true. I was nine years old, and I had better things to do with my time than sit around staring at a music book filled with tiny inscrutable black marks and trying to figure out which ones corresponded with which specific keys on the piano. As far as I was concerned, our piano had WAY too many keys on it anyway. I would have much preferred a piano with a total of two large keys, one white and one black; or maybe even just one really large gray key, so you'd never have any doubt which one you were supposed to hit.

But our piano had THOUSANDS of keys, stretching out for approximately a mile in either direction, and if I didn't hit *exactly the right one,* Mrs. Bat would make a federal case out of it. She'd stand over my shoulder and harangue me about sharps and flats for an HOUR—and in those days a Saturday hour was the equivalent of 53 weekday hours—until finally she'd give up and go outside to catch moths for dinner.

In other words, I was not a natural piano student, in stark contrast to Mozart, a brilliant musical prodigy who by age nine had already composed his classic work *Porgy and Bess.* I did eventually take up the guitar, and I even played in a band in college, but we didn't play complicated music. We played songs like "Land of 1,000 Dances," which only has one chord, namely, "E." In fact, a lot of our songs basically consisted of "E." Usually we'd play "E" for an hour or so, then we'd take a fifteen-minute break, during which we'd change over to "A."

So even though Lois Grant seemed to be a nice, sincere person, I frankly doubted that I had ever been Mozart, and I pretty much forgot about our correspondence until I received my copy of *Spirit at Work* and saw the chapter in there about me. I began to wonder: What if I really *was* the reincarnation of Mozart? I mean, I don't want to get too spiritual here, but if Joya/Michael is correct—if I really am the embodiment of one of the greatest musical minds in history—then anytime anybody plays any Mozart music, I should get royalties, right? So just to be on the safe side, if you use any of my songs—*The Marriage of Figaro, The Magic Flute,* "Summertime," "Happy Birthday," "Mony Mony," etc.—I'd appreciate it if you'd send me a check. Make it out to Dave "Wolfgang" Barry.

This photo of me with my son, Rob, was taken on the day I picked him up at junior high school in the Wienermobile, which the Oscar Mayer company had let me drive for a day. This was probably the most embarrassing moment of Rob's life. As a parent, I really enjoyed it.

NO RESPECT

A while ago the *New York Times* printed an item concerning an eleven-year-old girl who was overheard on the streets of East Hampton, New York, telling her father, "Daddy, Daddy, please don't sing!"

The daddy was Billy Joel.

The irony, of course, is that a lot of people would pay BIG money to hear Billy Joel sing. But of course these people are not Billy Joel's adolescent offspring. To his adolescent offspring, Billy Joel apparently represents the same thing that all parents represent to their adolescent offspring: Bozo-Rama. To an adolescent, there is nothing in the world more embarrassing than a parent.

When I was an adolescent, my dad wore one of those Russian-style hats that were semi-popular with middle-aged guys for a while in the early sixties. You may remember this hat: It was shaped kind of like those paper hats that some fast-food workers have to wear, only it was covered with fur. Nobody—and I include both Mel Gibson and the late Cary Grant in this statement—could wear this hat and not look like a complete dork.

So naturally my dad wore one. The fur on his was dark and curly; it looked as though this hat had been made from a poodle. My dad was the smartest, most decent, most perceptive person I've ever known, but he was a card-carrying member of the Fashion Club for Men Who Wear Bermuda Shorts with the Waist up Around Their Armpits, Not to Mention Sandals with Dark Socks.

My dad liked his Russian hat because he was bald and it kept him warm; he did not care what it looked like. But I cared *deeply*. I especially cared when I was waiting for my dad to pick me up outside Harold C. Crittenden Junior High School after canteen. Canteen was this school-sponsored youth activity designed to give us something to do on Friday nights other than vandalize mailboxes; we'd go to the school, and the boys would go to the gym to play basketball, while the girls went to the cafeteria to play "Please Mr. Postman" 700 consecutive times on the 45 rpm lo-fi record player and dance the Slop with each other. Eventually the boys would wander in from the gym, and the girls would put on slow, romantic songs such as "Put Your Head on My Shoulder," and the boys, feeling the first stirrings of what would one day grow and blossom into mature love, would pour soft drinks down each other's pants.

After canteen we'd stand outside the school, surrounded by our peers, waiting for our parents to pick us up; when my dad pulled up, wearing his poodle hat and driving his Nash Metropolitan—a comically tiny vehicle resembling those cars outside supermarkets that go up and down when you put in a quarter, except the Metropolitan looked sillier and had a smaller motor—I was mortified. I might as well have been getting picked up by a flying saucer piloted by some bizarre multitentacled stalk-eyed slobber-mouthed alien being that had somehow got hold of a Russian hat. I was horrified at what my peers might think of my dad; it never occurred to me that my peers didn't even notice my dad, because they were too busy being mortified by *their* parents.

Of course eventually my father stopped being a hideous embarrassment to me, and I, grasping the Torch of Dorkhood, became a hideous embarrassment to my son—especially when, like Billy Joel, I try to sing. (I don't mean that I try to sing like Billy Joel; I try to sing more like Aretha Franklin.) If you want to see a flagrant and spectacular violation of the known laws of physics, watch what my son does if we are in a public place and for some reason I need to burst into the opening notes of "Respect" ("WHAT you want! Baby I got it!"). When this happens, my son's body will instantaneously disappear into another dimension and rematerialize as far as two football fields away. The results are even more dramatic with the song "Got My Mojo Workin'."

Yes, parents: In the ongoing battle between you and your adolescent children, you possess the ultimate weapon—the Power to Embarrass. Use this power, parents! If your adolescent children are in ANY way displeasing you—if they are mouthing off or engaging in unacceptable behavior—do not waste your breath nagging them. Instead, simply do what Billy Joel and I do: sing. In fact, I think our judicial system should use this power to punish teenage criminal defendants:

> *Judge:* Young man, this is your third offense. I'm afraid I'm going to have to give you the maximum sentence.
> *Youthful Defendant:* No! Not . . .
> *Judge:* Yes. I'm going to ask your mom to get up here on the court karaoke machine and sing "Copacabana."

Youthful Defendant: NO! SEND ME TO PRISON! PLEASE!!

Yes, if we were to impose this kind of justice, we'd see a dramatic drop in adolescent crime. The streets would be safer, the adults would be in charge again, and the nation would be a happier place. Just thinking about it makes me want to sing a joyful song. Come on! Everybody join in!

Havin' my BABY!
What a lovely way of saying how much . . .

Hey! Where'd everybody go?

THE NAME GAME

I want to stress that I'm not bitter about what the Philip Morris Corporation is trying to do with the name "Dave."

In case you didn't know, Philip Morris is test-marketing a new brand of cigarettes called Dave's. Over the past year I've seen big billboard advertisements for Dave's cigarettes in Seattle and Denver. These are folksy ads; one of them features a tractor. The message is that Dave's is a folksy brand of cigarette, produced by a down-to-earth, tractor-driving guy named Dave for ordinary people who work hard and make an honest living, at least until they start coughing up big folksy chunks of trachea.

Of course there is no actual Dave. The people at Philip Morris are just calling the new brand Dave's because they think the name Dave sounds trustworthy and non-corporate. This is pretty funny when you consider that Philip Morris is the world's largest tobacco company and has enough marketing experts and advertising consultants and lawyers and lobbyists to sink an aircraft carrier, not that I'm suggesting anything.

According to an article in *Advertising Age*, Philip Morris made up a whole story—described by a Philip Morris spokesperson as "a tale of fictional imagery"—about how the Dave's brand of cigarettes got started. Here's the story, as quoted by *Advertising Age* from Philip Morris promotional materials:

"Down in Concord, N.C., there's a guy named Dave. He lives in the heart of tobacco farmland. Dave enjoys lots of land, plenty of freedom, and his yellow '57 pickup truck. Dave was fed up with cheap, fast-burning smokes. Instead of just getting mad, he did something about it . . . Dave's tobacco company was born."

Is that a heartwarming and inspirational tale of fictional imagery, or what? A guy—a regular guy: a guy exactly like you, except that he doesn't exist—gets FED UP with the status quo. So instead of just sitting around and complaining, he gets up off his imaginary butt and—in the great "can-do" tradition of Americans such as John Wayne, who courageously pretended to be many brave heroes before he died with just the one remaining lung—"Dave" decides to *make his own brand of cigarettes*.

Philip Morris does not provide details regarding how, exactly, Dave raised the money to build his cigarette factory. Maybe Dave robbed a nursing home; maybe Dave borrowed the money from other members of his neo-Nazi group; maybe Dave sold his huge collection of child pornography. You could make up any story you wanted about what Dave did, because Dave is not real! That's the kind of fun you and Philip Morris can have with tales of fictional imagery.

On the other hand, you must be very, very careful when you talk about real people. An example of a real person would be Geoffrey C. Bible, who is the chief executive officer of Philip Morris.

Because Geoffrey C. Bible is real, you should not use the name "Geoffrey C. Bible" in a derogatory way. You should not, for example, say, "Darn it! The dog made Geoffrey C. Bible on the carpet again!" Nor should you permit your youngsters to use expressions such as "Tommy stuck his finger way up into his nose and pulled out a big old Geoffrey C. Bible!" Nor should you say that a person caught engaging in an unnatural act of romance with a sheep was "doing the Geoffrey C. Bible." That would be wrong.

It would also be wrong to make up a tale of fictional imagery about Geoffrey C. Bible, such as:

"Down in the heart of Philip Morris corporate headquarters there's a guy named Geoffrey C. Bible. Geoffrey C. Bible enjoys plenty of employees and a corporate jet. Geoffrey C. Bible was fed up with so-called 'scientists' saying that cigarettes kill more people every year than alcohol, cocaine, crack, heroin, homicide, suicide, and O.J. Simpson. Instead of just getting mad, Geoffrey C. Bible did something about it. He deposited his enormous paycheck."

So does everybody understand the ethical point here? You may NOT take liberties with the name "Geoffrey C. Bible." You may, however, take the name "Dave" and do pretty much whatever you want to it. As I say, I'm not at all bitter that Philip Morris has decided to appropriate my name, and my father's name, and the name that a lot of regular guys who really exist have used over the years, a name that has apparently earned some measure of trust, which is why Philip Morris wants to attach its new cigarette brand to this name, the way a leech attaches itself to your leg. Who knows? If this strategy works out, maybe it'll inspire a whole bunch of new cigarette brands with trustworthy names. I bet that even as you read this, some marketing people, somewhere, are batting around the concept of "Jesus" cigarettes.

They need to keep coming up with ideas. They're in a tough business: The people who use their products—and I am NOT implying that there's a connection—keep dying of lung cancer. It's an unfortunate situation, and I for one am getting fed up. But instead of getting mad, I'm going to do something about it.

I'm going to start calling lung cancer "Geoffrey's disease."

BORN TO BE JERKS

Recently, when I was having a hamburger at an outdoor restaurant, two guys started up their Harley-Davidson motorcycles, parked maybe twenty-five feet from me.

Naturally, being Harley guys, these were rebels—lone wolves, guys who do it Their Way, guys who do not follow the crowd. You could tell because they were wearing the same jeans, jackets, boots, bandannas, sunglasses, belt buckles, tattoos, and (presumably) underwear worn by roughly 28 million other lone-wolf Harley guys.

And of course, once they got their engines started, they had to spend the equivalent of two college semesters just sitting there, revving their engines, which were so earbleedingly loud that I thought my hamburger was going to leap from my plate and skitter, terrified, back into the kitchen. I believe many Harley guys spend more time revving their engines than actually driving anywhere; I sometimes wonder why they bother to have wheels on their motorcycles.

Perhaps you, too, have experienced an assault of Harley-revving; and perhaps you have asked yourself: Why do these people DO this? What possible reason could they have for causing so much discomfort to those around them?

As it happens, there IS a reason, and it is an excellent one: They're jerks.

I'm not saying that ALL Harley guys—some of my friends are Harley guys—engage in this obnoxious behavior. I'm just saying that the ones who DO engage in it are jerks. And I am not afraid to tell them so, even if they are large and hairy and potentially violent. I am not afraid to say: "Okay, Mr. Loud Harley Guy, you got a problem with me calling you a jerk? You want to DO something about it? You want to express your disagreement by tapping out lengthy Morse code sentences on my skull with a tire iron? Then why don't you—if you have the guts—come see me PERSONALLY at my place of employment, located at 1600 Pennsylvania Avenue, Washington, D.C.? Come on if you dare, fat boy! Ride right into the lobby!"

And let me also say, while I'm at it, that I'm sick of you people who park in spaces reserved for the handicapped, even though you are not, personally, handicapped. You know who you are. Many of you even have those little rearview-mirror handicapped signs, which you got from a friend or relative, or which you once needed because of some temporary medical condition that has long since been cleared up.

One of my hobbies is to watch when cars pull into handicapped parking spots, and see who gets out. Very often, in my experience, these people appear to be totally unhandicapped: no wheelchair; no crutches; not even a trace of a limp. I realize that some of these people have problems, such as heart conditions, that are not visible. But some of them, to judge by the sprightliness of their walks, are off to compete in the decathlon. Their only handicap is: They're jerks.

What we need in this country—I would pay extra income tax for this—is an elite corps of Handicapped Parker On-Site Medical Examination SWAT Teams. These teams would prowl the streets, wearing rubber gloves and armed with X-ray machines, CAT scanners, scalpels, drills, saws, and harpoon-sized hypodermic needles.

When a team spotted a handicapped-zone parker who could not immediately prove that he or she was handicapped, that person would immediately undergo a severely thorough on-the-street physical examination conducted by burly personnel who have attended medical school for a maximum of four hours including lunch ("Hey Norm! Which ones are the kidneys again?"). These examinations would involve full frontal nudity and the removal of enough blood, organ, and tissue samples to form a complete new human; also, if the SWAT team found a Harley guy revving his engine in a handicapped-parking zone, it would employ the 250-foot intestinal probe nicknamed "Big Bertha." The idea would be that if you weren't qualified to park in a handicapped zone BEFORE the physical examination, you definitely would be AFTER.

And let's talk about you people who always send your food back in restaurants. (I KNOW this has nothing to do with handicapped parking; I can't stop myself.) I mean, sure, if the food is truly BAD, if it has RODENTS running around on it, okay, send it back; but what about you people who ALWAYS send your food back, thereby turning EVERY SINGLE MEAL into an exercise in consumer whining? I'm sorry! You're jerks! Especially if, when the bill comes, you also ALWAYS insist—even if everybody ordered basically the same thing—on figuring out your EXACT share ("Well, I had the Diet Sprite, which is ten cents less than the iced tea . . ."); and then you decide that a 5 percent tip is adequate, thereby forcing your friends, who are embarrassed, to put in more money.

Listen carefully to what I am about to tell you. Put your ear right down to the page:

YOUR FRIENDS HATE IT WHEN YOU STIFF THE WAITER. IF THE SERVICE IS OKAY, YOU SHOULD TIP 15 PERCENT. IF YOU DON'T WANT TO TIP, THEN DON'T EAT AT RESTAURANTS.

Also, you should never, ever, no matter what, butt in front of people waiting in line without asking their permission.

Also, if, when you talk to people, they keep backing away from you, it's because you're TOO CLOSE, all right? SO DON'T KEEP ADVANCING ON THEM LIKE A HUMAN GLACIER.

Thank you, and I apologize for using so many capital letters. I can be a real jerk about that.

THE PEOPLE'S COURT

Today, as part of my ongoing series entitled "Advancing Your Career," I'm going to address the often-asked question: Should you set fire to your supervisor's beard?

But first I need to formally apologize to the Harley-Davidson motorcycle riders for a column I wrote a couple of months ago in which I stated—without having done any research—that people who repeatedly rev their extremely loud Harley-Davidsons in crowded public places are jerks.

Well. You talk about stirring up a hornet's nest. I have not received so much irate mail since the time I criticized Neil Diamond.

(NOTE TO NEIL DIAMOND FANS: Please don't write to me again! I now worship Neil as a god! I have a graven image of him to which I ritually sacrifice goats!)

(NOTE TO ANIMAL-RIGHTS ACTIVISTS: I'm just kidding!)

(NOTE TO NEIL DIAMOND FANS: Not that I am saying Neil is not worthy of goat sacrifice!)

In their letters to me, the Harley-Davidson people made four basic points:

1. I am scum.
2. There are important mechanical and safety reasons why Harley-Davidson engines need to be extremely loud and revved a lot.
3. I am lower than scum.
4. Perhaps I would like to have my skull crushed like a Ping-Pong ball under a freight locomotive.

Here are some actual unretouched quotations from the letters I received:

- *"Dear mr Barry yes you are a looser and yes you are anal retentive."*
- *"You are an idiot! You should be writing you're so called journalism for National Inquirer."*
- *"My loud Harley might catch your attention from concentrating on singing your favorite Barry Manilow song."*
- *"I don't guess you know that lawyers, Doctors, country singers own Harley."*
- *"You (bleeping) polyester buying, penny loafer sporting, polka-dot tie wearing, bus riding, no life having (motherbleeper)."*

So I just want to make this sincere statement of apology to those Harley riders whom I have offended: Don't you EVER accuse me of listening to Barry Manilow.

(NOTE TO BARRY MANILOW FANS: Just kidding! I love Barry's work! Especially the Dr Pepper commercial!)

Okay, now that we've cleared that up, I want to share with you an item from a newsletter published by the Utah Department of Employment Security, sent to me by alert reader John Balmforth. The newsletter has a feature titled

YOU BE THE JUDGE, which presents a case concerning whether a company was justified in discharging an employee (referred to as the "claimant"). Here, according to the newsletter are the facts, as determined at a hearing:

- *"During a disciplinary discussion with his supervisor, the claimant lit the supervisor's beard on fire with a cigarette lighter."*
- *"Shortly thereafter, the claimant refused to follow instructions from his trainer and, when rebuked, the worker pressed a Post-it note on the trainer's forehead."*

Okay! You be the judge! Was the employer justified in firing this person? Think about it while we play the *Jeopardy* music:

Doo doo doo doo, doo doo doo, doo doo doo doo DOO doo-doo-doo-doo-doo . . .

Time's up! The answer, according to the Utah Department of Employment Security is: Yes, the employer WAS justified. The newsletter points out that "not only is setting a person's beard on fire dangerous," but also the forehead Post-it note indicates "an absence of professional behavior." The department apparently did not give the employee any credit for refraining from attaching the note with a stapler.

Speaking of assaults, I have here a chilling news item from the September 3 edition of the *Asbury Park Press*, alertly sent in by John F. Coffey II, attorney at law. The item, which was written by Sheri Tabachnik and which I am not making up, begins as follows:

"A Belmar man who was throwing uncooked pasta out the window was charged by police with stabbing a man who was hit by the rigatoni, police said."

The article states that the victim and some friends were walking on the street at about 2 A.M. when "some people in an apartment began throwing uncooked pasta out the window at them." Words were exchanged, and the pasta-wielding perpetrator allegedly came out of the apartment and stabbed the victim. According to a police spokesperson, "He must have hit him in an artery because he was gushing blood."

The victim survived, but this tragic incident serves as yet another reminder to us all that, when we feel stress or anger, we must NOT, in a rash moment, unthinkingly reach for the rigatoni. Instead we should remember the words of the great pacifist Mohandas Gandhi, who in a famous 1949 speech, said, "Me, I prefer the number nine capellini." What is all the more amazing about this speech is that Gandhi actually died in 1948.

So in conclusion, let me just reiterate my main points, which are (1) it is unprofessional to set fire to our supervisors, at least in Utah; (2) when pasta is outlawed, only outlaws will have pasta; and (3) we should not be critical of people who make extremely loud motorcycle noises in public if we are sporting penny loafers. And now, if you'll excuse me, I'm going to go listen to "I Write the Songs."

TUNED IN, TUNED OFF

So I turned on my car radio, and the first thing I heard was the Shouting Car-Dealership Jerk. You know the one I mean. He sounds like this:

"BELOW DEALER COST!! MAX SNOTWICK FORD DODGE ISUZU CHEVROLET NISSAN STUDEBAKER TOYOTA IS SELLING CARS AT BELOW DEALER COST!! WE'RE LOSING MONEY ON THESE CARS!! WE HAVE TO MAKE ROOM FOR MORE CARS!! SO WE CAN LOSE MORE MONEY!! WE HAVE PROCESSED CHEESE FOR BRAINS!! THAT'S WHY WE'RE SELLING CARS FOR BELOW DEALER . . ."

I immediately did what I always do when the Shouting Car-Dealership Jerk comes on: I changed the station. I will listen to *anything*—including Morse code, static, and the song "A Horse with No Name"—before I will listen to those commercials, and I think most people feel the same way. So the question is: Why are they on the air? Why are car dealerships paying good money for commercials that people hate?

My theory is that these commercials are NOT paid for by

car dealerships; they're paid for by competing radio stations, who hope you'll switch to them. I developed a similar theory years ago to explain the infamous "ring around the collar" TV commercials for Wisk. Remember those? They always featured a Concerned Housewife who tried and tried to get her husband's collars clean; but when her husband, who apparently did not wash his neck, would put on a shirt, people would point out that his collar was dirty. You'd think he'd have punched them in the mouth, but instead he just looked chagrined, and these extremely irritating voices—voices that would kill a laboratory rat in seconds—would shriek: "RING AROUND THE COLLAR! RING AROUND THE COLLAR!" And the Concerned Housewife would be SO embarrassed that the only thing preventing her from lying down right on her kitchen floor and slashing her wrists was the fear that the paramedics might notice that she had waxy yellow buildup.

There was a time when the "ring around the collar" campaign was arguably the single most detested aspect of American culture. Many people swore that, because of those commercials, they would not purchase Wisk if it were the last detergent on Earth. Yet the commercials stayed on the air for *years*. Why? Because *somebody* was buying Wisk. The question is: Who?

My theory is that it was the Soviet Union. These ads ran during the height of the Cold War, when the Soviets would stop at nothing to destroy America. I believe they sent agents over here with the mission of purchasing huge quantities of Wisk; this convinced the Wisk manufacturers that the "ring around the collar" campaign was working, so they kept it on the air, thereby causing millions of Americans to conclude that they lived in a nation of complete idiots, and thus to become depressed and alienated. I believe that virtually all the negative developments of the sixties and seventies—riots, protests, crime, drug use, *The Gong Show*— were related, directly or indirectly, to Wisk commercials. I also believe that to this day, somewhere in the former Soviet Union, there are giant hidden underground caverns containing millions of bottles of Wisk.

I'll tell you another kind of ad I hate: The ones where they give you information that could never be of any conceivable use to you. For example, there was a series of ads for some giant chemical company, I forget which one, where they'd show you, say, a family watching television, and the announcer would say something like: "We don't make televisions. And we don't make the little plastic things that hold the wires inside the televisions. We make the machines that stamp the numbers on the little plastic things that hold the wires inside the televisions." When I saw those ads, I wanted to scream: WHY ARE YOU PAYING MILLIONS OF DOLLARS TO TELL ME THIS?? WHAT DO YOU WANT ME TO DO??

I also do not care for:

- Any ad featuring a demonstration of a product absorbing an intimate bodily fluid.
- Any ad where a singer sings with deep emotion about something nobody could possibly feel deeply emotional about, such as cotton, Hoover vacuum cleaners, and Jiffy Lube. Builders Square has a commercial wherein the singer bleats this hyperpatriotic song that makes it sound as though the people shopping there are actually building America, whereas in fact they are looking for replacement toilet parts.

- Any of the endless series of ads by long-distance companies accusing other long-distance companies of lying. LISTEN, LONG-DISTANCE COMPANIES: WE DON'T BELIEVE ANY OF YOU ANYMORE. WE'RE THINKING OF GOING BACK TO SMOKE SIGNALS.

Excuse me for shouting like the Car Dealership Jerk; I get emotional about this. I'm sure you do, too, which is why I'm inviting you to write to me at One Herald Plaza, Miami, FL 33132, and tell me—BRIEFLY—what advertisements, past or present, that you really hate, and why. I'll write a column about this, which will benefit humanity in general by enabling me to write yet another column without doing any research. Don't thank me: I do it all for you. At WAY below dealer cost.

SNUGGLE BEAR MUST DIE!

Whew! Do I have a headache! I think I'll take an Extra Strength Bufferin Advil Tylenol with proven cavity fighters, containing more of the lemon-freshened borax and plaque fighters for those days when I am feeling "not so fresh" in my personal region!

The reason I'm feeling this way is that I have just spent six straight days going through the thousands of letters you readers sent in when I asked you to tell me which advertisements you don't like. It turns out that a lot of you really, REALLY hate certain advertisements, to the point where you fantasize about acts of violence. For example, quite a few people expressed a desire to kill the stuffed bear in the Snuggle fabric-softener commercial. "Die, Snuggle Bear! Die!" is how several put it.

Likewise there was a great deal of hostility expressed, often by older readers, toward the relentlessly cheerful older couples depicted in the competing commercials for Ensure and Sustacal. These commercials strongly suggest that if you drink these products, you will feel "young," which, in these commercials, means "stupid." People were particularly offended by the commercial where the couple actually drinks a *toast* with Ensure. As Jamie Hagedorn described it: "One says, 'To your health,' and the other says, 'Uh-uh—to OUR health,' and then for some reason they laugh like ninnies. I want to hit them both over the head with a hammer."

Some other commercial personalities who aroused great hostility were Sally Struthers; the little boy who lectures you incessantly about Welch's grape juice; the young people in the Mentos commercials (as Rob Spore put it, "Don't you think those kids should all be sent to military school?"); everybody in all Calvin Klein commercials ("I am sure they are what hell is really like," observed Robert E. Waller); the little girl in the Shake 'N Bake commercial—Southerners REALLY hate this little girl—who, for what seemed like hundreds of years, said "And I helped!" but pronounced it "An ah hayulpt!" (Louise Sigmund, in a typically restrained response, wrote, "Your mother shakes chickens in hell"); Kathie Lee Gifford (Shannon Saar wrote, "First person to push Kathie Lee overboard gets an all-you-can-eat buffet!"); the smug man in the Geritol commercial who said, "My wife, I think I'll keep her!" (the wife smiled, but you just know that one day she will put Liquid Drāno in his Ensure); the bad actor pretending to be Dean Witter in the flagrantly fake "old film" commercial that's supposed to make us want to trust them with our money; the woman in the Pantene commercial who said "Please don't hate me because I'm beautiful" (as many readers responded, "Okay, how about if we just hate you because you're obnoxious?").

Also they are none too fond of the giant Gen X dudes stomping all over the Rocky Mountains in the Coors Light ads. (Matt Scott asks: "Will they step on us if we don't buy their beer?" Scott McCullar asks: "What happens when they get a full bladder?")

Also, many people would like Candice Bergen to just shut up about the stupid dimes.

Also, I am pleased to report that I am not the only person who cannot stand the sight of the Infiniti Snot—you know, the guy with the dark clothes and the accent, talking about Infiniti cars as though they were Renaissance art. As Kathleen Schon, speaking for many, put it: "We hate him so much we wouldn't buy one even if we could afford it, which we can't, but we wouldn't buy one anyway."

Speaking of car commercials, here's a bulletin for the Nissan people: Nobody likes the creepy old man, okay? Everybody is afraid when the little boy winds up alone in the barn with him. This ad campaign does not make us want to purchase a Nissan. It makes us want to notify the police. Thank you.

And listen, Chevrolet: People didn't mind the first 389 million times they heard Bob Seger wail "Like a rock!" But it's getting old. And some people wish to know what "genuine Chevrolet" means. As Don Charleston put it, "I intended to buy a genuine Chevy but I couldn't tell the difference between the 'genuine' and all those counterfeit Chevys out there, so I bought a Ford."

But the car-related ads that people hate the most, judging from my survey, are the dealership commercials in which the announcer SHOUTS AT YOU AS THOUGH YOU ARE AN IDIOT and then, in the last three seconds of the ad reads, in very muted tones, what sounds like the entire U.S. tax code. Hundreds and hundreds of people wrote to say they hate these commercials. I should note that one person defended them: His name is George Chapogas, and he is in—of all things—the advertising business. Perhaps by examining this actual excerpt from his letter, we can appreciate the thinking behind the shouting ads:

"I write, produce and VOICE those ads. Make a damn good living doing it, too. Maybe more than you even. And would you like to know why? Because they move metal, buddy."

Thanks, George! I understand now.

Well, I'm out of space. Tune in next week, and I'll tell you which commercial the readers hated the most; I'll also discuss repulsive bodily functions in detail. Be sure to read it! You'll lose weight without dieting, have whiter teeth in two weeks by actually growing your own hair on itching, flaking skin as your family enjoys this delicious meal in only minutes without getting soggy in milk! Although your mileage may vary. Ask a doctor! Or somebody who plays one on TV.

WHUPPING
MR. WHIPPLE

L ast week I promised that in today's column I would announce which commercial, according to my survey, you readers hate the most. So if you have an ounce of sense or good taste, you'll stop reading this column right now.

Really, I mean it . . .

This is your last chance . . .

You're making a HUGE mistake . . .

Okay, you pathetic fool: The most hated commercial of all time, according to the survey, was the one for Charmin featuring "Mr. Whipple" and various idiot housewives who lived in a psycho pervert community where everybody was obsessed with squeezing toilet paper—or, as they say in Commercial Land, "bathroom tissue." Americans still, after all these years, feel more hostility toward that ad campaign than they ever did toward international communism.

Of course some people will say: "But those ads sold a lot of Charmin!"

Yes, and the Unabomber produced high-quality, handcrafted letter bombs. But that doesn't make it *right*.

The Mr. Whipple ads are related to a whole category of

commercials that, according to the survey, people really detest—namely, commercials that discuss extremely intimate bodily functions and problems, often at dinnertime. People do not wish to hear total strangers blurting out statements about their constipation and their diarrhea and their hemorrhoids and their "male itch." People do not wish to see scientific demonstrations of pads absorbing amazing quantities of fluids. People also cannot fathom why this fluid is always blue. As Carla and Bill Chandler put it: "If anyone around here starts secreting anything BLUE, the last thing we're going to worry about is how absorbent their pad is."

People do not wish to hear any more about incontinence. Rich Klinzman wrote: "I have often fantasized about sneaking up behind June Allyson, blowing up a paper bag, and slamming my fist into it, just to see how absorbent those adult diapers really are."

People also do not wish to see actors pretending to be mothers and daughters talking about very personal feminine matters as though they were discussing the weather. Richard J. O'Neil, expressing a common sentiment, wrote: "If I was a woman, I would walk on my lips through a sewage plant before I would share this kind of information with any living soul, let alone my mother."

People do not wish to see extreme close-ups of other people chewing.

People are also getting mighty tired of the endlessly escalating, extremely confusing war of the pain relievers. At one time, years ago, there was just aspirin, which was basically for headaches; now, there are dozens of products, every single one of which seems to be telling you that, not only is it more *effective* than the other ones, but also the other ones could cause a variety of harmful side effects such as death. It seems safer to just live with the headache.

Many survey respondents were especially scornful of the commercials suggesting that you can undergo an actual surgical procedure, such as a Caesarean section, and the only pain medication you'd need afterward is Tylenol. As Gwen Marshall put it: "If my doctor had given me Tylenol and expected me to be pain-free and happy, I'd have jumped off of that lovely table that holds your legs ten feet apart, grabbed the twelve-inch scalpel out of his hand, and held it to his throat until I got morphine, lots of it."

Another type of advertising that people detest is the Mystery Commercial, in which there is no earthly way to tell what product is being advertised. These commercials usually consist of many apparently random images flashing rapidly past on the screen, and then, at the end, you see a Nike swoosh, or the IBM logo, or Mr. Whipple.

People are sick and tired of seeing actors pretend to be deeply emotionally attached to their breakfast cereals. People also frankly do not believe that the woman in the Special K commercials got to be thin and shapely by eating Special K. Patricia Gualdoni wrote: "I have eaten enough Special K cereal to sink a battleship, and I look a lot more like a battleship than the woman in the ad."

People are also skeptical of the Denorex shampoo commercials. "How do we know that that tingling sensation isn't battery acid eating through your scalp?" asked Alyssa Church.

Here are just a few of the other views expressed by the thousands of readers who responded to the survey:

—Andy Elliott wrote: "I hate radio ads that say, 'Our

prices are so low, we can't say them on the radio!' WHY??? Will people start bleeding from the ears if they hear these prices?"

—Michael Howard wrote: "I live near Seattle and there is one channel that runs commercials approximately every five minutes advertising the fact that they have a helicopter. Can you believe it? A *helicopter!*"

—A.J. VanHorn theorized that "the increase in suicides among young people is due to the beer commercial showing a bunch of rednecks in a beat-up pickup swigging beer from cans and telling everyone 'It don't git no better'n this.' "

—Kathy Walden objected to "Wal-Mart commercials that shamelessly try to portray all Wal-Mart customers as poor, uneducated, rural, and concerned primarily with reproducing themselves. Of course this is true, but STILL . . ."

There were many, many more strong comments, but I'm out of space. So I'm going to close with a statement penned by a reader identifying himself as "Flat Foot Sam," who I believe spoke for millions of consumers when he wrote these words:

I'd like to buy the world a Coke,
And spray it out my nose.

Here I am kissing a horse named Sid, on which I sat during a celebrity polo match in Florida. The other celebrities' horses galloped up and down the field chasing the ball, but Sid just stood still the entire time. I was really grateful to him.

BEWARE THE EAGLE EYE

It's time once again for our popular consumer health feature, "You Should Be More Nervous."

Today we're going to address an alarming new trend, even scarier in some ways than the one we discussed several years ago concerning the danger of airplane toilets sucking out your intestines (if you had forgotten about that one, we apologize for bringing it up again, and we ask you to please put it out of your mind).

We were made aware of this new menace when alert reader Edna Aschenbrenner sent us an item from an Enterprise, Oregon, newspaper called—get ready for a great newspaper name—*The Wallowa County Chieftain*. The *Chieftain* runs a roundup of news from the small town of Imnaha (suggested motto: "It's 'Ahanmi' Spelled Backward!"). On March 14, this roundup, written by Barbara Kriley, began with the following story, which I am not making up:

"A bald eagle sabotaged the Imnaha power line for an hour and a half outage Wednesday with a placenta from the Hubbard Ranch calving operation. The eagle dropped the afterbirth across the power lines, effectively shorting out the power."

This is a truly alarming story. We're talking about a *bald eagle*, the proud symbol of this great nation as well as Budweiser beer. We don't know about you, but we always *trusted* eagles; we assumed that when they were soaring majestically across the skies, they were *protecting* us—scanning the horizon, keeping an eye out for storm fronts, Russian missiles, pornography, etc. But now we find out, thanks to the *Chieftain*, that they're not protecting us at all: They're up there dropping cow placentas. They've already demonstrated that they can take out the Imnaha power supply; it would be child's play for them to hit a human.

Nobody is safe. Can you imagine what would happen to our democratic system of government if, just before election day, one of the leading presidential contenders, while speaking at an outdoor rally, were to be struck on the head by a cow afterbirth traveling at 120 miles per hour?

Nothing, that's what would happen. First off, your presidential contenders do not ever stop speaking for any reason, including unconsciousness. Second, they're used to wearing ridiculous headgear to garner support from some headgear-wearing group or another. It would be only a matter of time before ALL the leading contenders were sporting cow placentas.

But a direct hit could have a disastrous effect on ordinary taxpayers. That is why we are issuing the following urgent plea to the personnel at the Hubbard Ranch and every other calving operation within the sound of our voice: PLEASE DO NOT LEAVE UNATTENDED PLACENTAS LYING AROUND. This is especially important if you see eagles loitering nearby, trying to look bored, smoking cigarettes, acting as though they could not care less. Please dispose of your placentas in the manner prescribed by the U.S. Surgeon General; namely, mail them, in secure packaging, to *The Ricki Lake Show.* Thank you.

We wish we could tell you that the Imnaha attack was an isolated incident, but we cannot—not in light of a news item from the *Detroit Free Press,* written by Kate McKee and sent in by many alert readers, concerning a Michigan man who was struck in an extremely sensitive area—you guessed it; his rental car—by a five-pound sucker fish falling from the sky. I am also not making this up. The man, Bob Ringewold, was quoted as saying that the fish was dropped by a "young eagle." (The article doesn't say how he knew the eagle was young; maybe it was wearing a little baseball cap backward.) The fish dented the roof of the car, although Ringewold was not charged for the damage (this is why you car renters should always take the Optional Sucker Fish Coverage).

And here comes the bad news: This is NOT the scariest recent incident involving an airborne fish. We have here an Associated Press item, sent in by many alert readers, which begins:

"A Brazilian fisherman choked to death near the remote Amazon city of Belem after a fish unexpectedly jumped into his mouth."

The item—we are still not making any of these items up—states that "the six-inch-long fish suddenly leapt out of the river" while the fisherman "was in the middle of a long yawn."

Of course this could be simply a case of a fish—possibly a young fish, inexperienced or on drugs—not paying attention to where it was going and jumping into somebody's mouth. On the other hand, it could be something much more ominous. It could be that fish in general, after thousands of years of being hounded by fishermen and dropped on rental cars, are finally deciding to fight back in the only way they know how.

If so, there is trouble ahead. You know those Saturday-morning professional-bass-fishing programs on TV? We should start monitoring those programs closely, because the fish on those programs are probably SICK AND TIRED of always playing the role of victims. It is only a matter of time before there is a situation where a couple of televised angling professionals are out on a seemingly peaceful lake, casting their lures, and they happen to yawn, and suddenly the water erupts in fury as dozens of vengeful bass launch themselves like missiles and deliberately lodge themselves deep into every available angler orifice. And we would NOT want to miss that.

BRAIN SLUDGE

Today, as part of our series "The Human Brain, So to Speak," we explore the phenomenon of: Brain Sludge.

"Brain sludge" is a term coined by leading scientists to describe the vast collection of moronic things that your brain chooses to remember instead of useful information.

For example: Take any group of 100 average Americans, and sing to them, "Come and listen to my story 'bout a man named Jed." At least 97 of them will immediately sing: "A poor mountaineer, barely kept his family fed." They will sing this even if they are attending a funeral. They can't help it.

This particular wad of sludge—known to scientists as *The Beverly Hillbillies Theme Song Wad*—is so firmly lodged in the standard American brain lobe that it has become part of our national DNA, along with the *Gilligan's Island* wad. If a newborn American infant were abandoned in the wilderness and raised by wolves without any human contact or language, there would nevertheless come a day when he or she would blurt out, without having any idea what it meant: "A THREE-hour tour!" And the wolves would sing along. That's how pervasive brain sludge is.

What is the root of this problem? Like most human defects, such as thigh fat, the original cause is your parents. Soon after you were born, your parents noticed that you were, functionally, an idiot, as evidenced by the fact that you spent most of your waking hours trying to eat your own feet. So they decided to put something into your brain, but instead of information you'd actually *need* later in life— for example, the PIN number to your ATM card—they sang drivel to you, the same drivel that parents have been dumping into their children's brains since the Middle Ages, such as "Pop Goes the Weasel," "Itsy Bitsy Spider," and "Jeremiah Was a Bullfrog." Your parents thought they were stimulating your mind, but in fact they were starting the sludge-buildup process, not realizing that every cretinous word they put into your brain would stay there FOREVER, so that decades later you'd find yourself waking up in the middle of the night wondering: *Why? WHY did she cut off their tails with a carving knife?*

But your parents aren't the real problem. The REAL problem, the nuclear generator of brain sludge, is television. Here's a little test for those readers out there who are approximately forty-eight years old. How many of you know what the Fourth Amendment to the Constitution says? Let's see those hands ... one ... two ... Okay, I count nine people. Now, how many of you remember the theme song to the 1950s TV show *Robin Hood*? Thousands of you! Me too! Everybody join in:

Robin Hood, Robin Hood riding through the glen!
Robin Hood, Robin Hood, with his band of men!
Feared by the bad! Loved by the good!
Robin Hood! Robin Hood! Robin Hood!

My brain also contains theme songs to early TV shows about Daniel Boone ("Daniel Boone was a man, yes a BIG man!"); Zorro ("The fox so cunning and free! He makes the sign of the Z!"); and Bat Masterson ("He wore a cane and derby hat! They called him Bat!").

I am not proud of this, but I can name only five Supreme Court Justices (one of whom sticks in my mind solely because of the term "pubic hair"); whereas I can name six Mousketeers.

Of course the densest layer of sludge consists of commercial jingles for products that no longer exist. Your brain assigns the highest priority to these. That's why, although I honestly cannot name the current secretary of defense, I can sing:

Pamper, Pamper, new shampoo!
Gentle as a lamb, so right for you!
Gentle as a lamb? YES, ma'am!
Pamper, Pamper, new shampoo!

My brain also loves to remind me that my beer is Rheingold, the dry beer; think of Rheingold whenever you buy beer! Brush-a, brush-a, brush-a! New Ipana toothpaste! With the brand-new flavor! It's dandy for your teeeeeeth!

Here's how pathetic my brain is: If it *forgets* some worthless piece of brain sludge, it drops everything else and becomes obsessed with *recalling* it. For example, right now my brain is devoting all available resources to remembering the name of the candy featured in the following jingle:

(NAME OF CANDY) goes a long, long way!
If you have one head, it lasts all day!

This is currently my brain's Manhattan Project; it will think of nothing else. A lot of people have this problem, and society pays a price for it:

> *Control Tower: Flight 8376, you're descending way too . . .*
> *Pilot: Tower, could you settle something? Was it* (singing) *"Brylcreem, a little bit'll do ya?"*
> *Tower: No, it was* (singing) *"a little dab'll do ya."*
> *Co-Pilot: Hah! Told you so!*
> *Pilot: Tower, are you sure?*
> *Tower: Definitely, "dab." Now about your descent rate . . . Hello? Flight 8376? HELLO?*

Yes, brain sludge is a leading cause of needless tragedy, which is why I'm asking you to join in the fight against it. How? Simple: Write a letter to senators and congresspersons DEMANDING that they appropriate $500 million for a study to for God's sake find out what kind of candy lasts all day if you have one head. And if there is any money left over, we should hire professional assassins to track down whoever wrote:

My bologna has a first name! It's . . .

BANG
Thank you.

DUDE, READ ALL ABOUT IT!

Here in the newspaper industry (official motto: "For Official Motto, Please Turn to Section F, Page 37") we are seriously worried. Newspaper readership is declining like crazy. In fact, there's a good chance that nobody is reading this column. I could write a pornographic sex scene here and nobody would notice.

"Oh Dirk," moaned Camille as she writhed nakedly on the bed. "Yes yes yes YES YES YES YES YESSSSSSSSSS!"

"Wait up!" shouted Dirk. "I'm still in the bathroom!"

It was not always this way. There was a time in America when everybody read newspapers. Big cities had spunky lads standing on every street corner shouting "EXTRA!" These lads weren't selling newspapers: They just shouted "EXTRA!" because they wanted to irritate people, and boomboxes had not been invented yet.

But the point is that in those days, most people read newspapers, whereas today, most people do not. What caused this change?

One big factor, of course, is that people are a lot stupider than they used to be, although we here in the newspaper industry would never say so in print.

Certainly another factor is that many people now get their news from television. This is unfortunate. I do not mean to be the slightest bit critical of TV news people, who do a superb job, considering that they operate under severe time constraints and have the intellectual depth of hamsters. But TV news can only present the "bare bones" of a story; it takes a newspaper, with its capability to present vast amounts of information, to render the story truly boring.

But if we want to identify the "root cause" of the decline in newspaper readership, I believe we have to point the finger of blame at the foolish decision by many newspapers to stop running the comic strip *Henry*. Remember Henry? The bald boy who looks like Dwight Eisenhower? I believe that readers liked the *Henry* strip because, in times of change and uncertainty, it always had the same plot:

Panel One: Henry is walking along the street. He is wearing shorts, even if it is winter.

Panel Two: Suddenly Henry spies an object. You can tell he's spying it, because a dotted line is going from his eyeball to the object. Often the object is a pie cooling on a windowsill (pies are always cooling on windowsills on the planet where Henry lives).

Panel Three: Things get really wacky as Henry eats the pie.

Panel Four: The woman who baked the pie comes to the window and discovers that—prepare to roll on the floor—*the pie is gone.* The woman is surprised. You can tell because exclamation points are shooting out of her head.

This timeless humor has been delighting readers for thousands of years (*Henry* strips have been found on prehistoric cave walls), but for some reason, a while back most newspapers stopped running the strip, and readership has been in the toilet ever since. I don't think it's a coincidence.

Whatever the cause, the readership decline is producing major underarm dampness here in the newspaper industry. We're especially concerned about the fact that we're losing young readers—the so-called Generation X, which gets its name from the fact that it followed the so-called Generation W. We're desperate to attract these readers. Go to any newspaper today and you'll see herds of editors pacing around, mooing nervously, trying to think up ways to make newspapers more relevant to today's youth culture. This is pretty funny if you know anything about newspaper editors, the vast majority of whom are middle-aged Dockers-wearing white guys who cannot recognize any song recorded after "Yellow Submarine."

But they're trying. If you read your newspaper carefully, you'll notice that you're seeing fewer stories with uninviting, incomprehensible, newspaper-ese headlines like *PANEL NIXES TRADE PACT*, and more punchy, "with-it" headlines designed to appeal to today's young people, like *PANEL NIXES TRADE PACT, DUDE.*

I applaud this effort, and as a middle-aged Dockers-wearing white guy, I want to do my part by making my column more "hep" and appealing to young people. So I'm going to conclude by presenting the views of some students of Daniel Kennedy's English class at Clearfield (Pennsylvania) Area High School. I recently wrote a column in which I said that some young people today have unattractive haircuts and don't know who Davy Crockett was. Mr.

Kennedy's class read this column and wrote me letters in response; here are some unretouched excerpts, which I am not making up:

- *"Maybe one of these days, you should look in the mirror, Dave. Dave, you need a new hairstyle, man! You have a puff-cut, Dave."*
- *"Without hair I think every guy in the world would just die of imbarresment. I know I would, but I am a girl."*
- *"You say that I don't no any thing about Davy Crockett. Well I no that he fought at the Alamo. He also played in several movies."*

Let me just say that we in the newspaper industry totally agree with you young people on these points and any other points you wish to make, and if you will please please PLEASE start reading the newspaper we'll be your best friend, okay? Okay? Young people? Hello?

You're not even reading this, you little twerps.

"Oh Dirk," moaned Camille, *"I am overcome by desire at the sight of your . . . your . . . What do you call those?"*

"Dockers," said Dirk.

INVASION OF THE TREE SHEEP

*C*all me paranoid, but my first reaction, upon learning about the dead sheep being found in treetops in New Zealand, was that something unusual was going on.

I found out about this thanks to alert reader Steven Moe, who sent me an article from *The Press* of Christchurch, New Zealand, concerning "the discovery of several dead sheep high in the trees of Tunnicliffe Forest."

Right away I said to myself: "Hmm." I base this statement on the well-known fact that sheep are not tree-dwelling animals. Zoologically, sheep are classified in the same family as cows: Animals That Stand Around and Poop. On very rare occasions, a single sheep or cow will climb a tree in an effort to escape a fierce natural predator such as a wolf or (around lunchtime) Luciano Pavarotti. But *The Press* article states that "four or five decomposing sheep were high in the branches." That is too many sheep to be explained by natural causes. Which leads us to the obvious explanation: namely, supernatural causes.

I realize that many of you laugh at stories of the paranormal. "Ha ha," you say. But the truth is that the world is full of strange phenomena that cannot be explained by the laws of logic or science. Dennis Rodman is only one example. There are many other documented cases of baffling supernatural occurrences. Consider these examples:

- *Early in the morning of October 8, 1991, Mrs. Florence A. Snegg of Uvula, Michigan, was having an extremely vivid dream in which her son, Russell, was involved in a terrible automobile accident. Suddenly she was awakened by the ringing of her telephone. On the line was a Missouri state trooper, calling long distance to remind Mrs. Snegg that she had never had children.*

- *On the afternoon of March 13, 1993, Winchester B. Fleen of Toad Sphincter, Arkansas, was abducted by hostile, large-brained beings who drilled holes in his head, probed him with giant needles, pumped chemicals into his body, took samples of his organs, and removed most of his bodily fluids before they found out that he did not have health insurance, at which point they released him back into the hospital waiting room.*

- *On the morning of July 3, 1994, seven-year-old Jason Toastwanker fell off his tricycle, hit his head, and was knocked out. When he regained consciousness, he spoke to his parents* in fluent German. *This did not surprise them, because they were Germans and this happened in Germany. What surprised them was that, before the accident, he had cleaned up his room* without being asked.

- *On February 12 of this year, Thelma Crumpet-Scone of New York City purchased a Whopper at Burger King; when she started to eat it, she bit her own finger, causing a painful red mark for several minutes. Incredibly, she decided that this was* totally her fault, *and she* did not sue anybody.

Impossible, you say? Perhaps so, but all of these incidents, along with hundreds more that have not occurred to me yet, have been thoroughly documented by the Institute for Documenting Things Thoroughly. The lesson is this: Before you say something is "impossible," you would be wise to remember the old saying: "Truth is stranger than fiction, especially when 'truth' is being defined by the O.J. Simpson defense team." And thus when you consider the New Zealand tree-sheep article, the question you must ask yourself is: "How can I, keeping an open mind, best explain what happened?"

The answer is: "Read the rest of the article, you moron." It turns out that the sheep had fallen from a helicopter. The pilot had been transporting—I am not making up this quote—"some ewes that had died from sleepy sickness," and the wire that was holding the sheep under the helicopter broke. Incredibly, the pilot had been warned about this the night before in a telephone call from a Missouri state trooper.

No, I made that last part up. But the rest of the story is true, which raises the following alarming questions for those who live in, or plan to visit, New Zealand:

- *Is it a common practice there to transport deceased sheep via helicopter?*
- *If one of these sheep were to land on you, would you get "sleepy sickness"?*
- *What about Mad Cow Disease?*

For the record, tree sheep are not the only bizarre phenomenon to occur lately in New Zealand. I have here a document, sent in by alert reader Gretl Collins, stating that a researcher in New Zealand has discovered a new, improved method for growing tomatoes hydroponically. ("Hydroponically" comes from the Greek words "hydro," meaning "a," and "ponically," meaning "way of growing tomatoes.") According to the document, the researcher has found that he gets excellent results when he grows the tomatoes in: brassieres. I am not making this up. This leads to still MORE questions, including:

- *Does this give new meaning to the expression "Get a load of those tomatoes"?*
- *Would it be tasteless to make a joke here about growing zucchini in athletic supporters?*
- *What about Mad Tomato Disease?*

There's probably nothing to worry about, but until we get some answers, I think everybody should panic for a while and then get some sleep. I myself am suddenly feeling VERY sleepy, so I'm just going to put my head down and . . .

Moo.

FOOD FIGHT

Today we present another part of our ongoing series, "Stuff That Guys Do."

Our first example of guys doing stuff comes from the *University of Washington Daily,* which on February 27 published a report written by Jeremy Simer and sent in by alert reader Donna Bellinger, headlined "Fraternity Game Turns Into Arrest."

What happened, according to this report, was that some guys were up on the roof of the Theta Delta Chi fraternity house, and, as guys will do when they spend any time together in an elevated location, they began sharing their innermost feelings.

I am of course kidding. These guys, being guys, began dropping things off the roof, starting with smaller items, and eventually escalating—this is when the police were summoned—to a chair and a rowing machine.

A fraternity member is quoted as follows: "We're frat guys. What can you say?"

Far be it from me to indulge in sex stereotyping here, but I am willing to bet that the reaction of you readers to this story is divided along gender lines, as follows:

Female Reaction: "Why would anybody do anything so STUPID?"
Male Reaction: "A rowing machine! COOL!"

The simple truth is that guys have this overpowering urge to watch stuff fall and crash. If you ever see an inappropriate object, such as a piano, hurtling toward the Earth from a great height, you can be virtually certain that guys are responsible.

Ask yourself this question: If you were standing in the middle of a bridge spanning a magnificent wilderness gorge, at the bottom of which was a spectacular whitewater river, what would you do?

Female Response: Admire the view.
Male Response: Spit.

Yes, the truth is that there are few things that a guy enjoys more than proudly watching a gob of spit—HIS spit; spit that HE produced—falling a tremendous distance. This is a male impulse that females frankly cannot relate to, just as males cannot relate to the female impulse to go into greeting-card stores and spend hours shopping for greeting cards even when there is no particular occasion or person you need to send a greeting card to, which is what women frequently do when guys are out spitting.

I am not suggesting here that all guys ever do is drop stuff. Sometimes they also throw stuff, and sometimes this can lead to trouble. I have in my possession an official U.S. government memorandum, sent to me by an alert but anonymous reader, that was written last year by Paul E.

Thompson, acting director, Western Region, Inspection Operations, Food and Safety Inspection Service, United States Department of Agriculture.

Here is the first paragraph of this memorandum, which I absolutely swear I am not making up:

"This is to remind all personnel of the danger and inadvisability of engaging in activities commonly referred to as 'Horseplay.' A few examples of horseplay include, but are not limited to: throwing spleens, squirting water, and flipping lymph nodes."

In professional journalism, we have an old saying that we frequently say, which goes like this: "You do not print a story about federal employees engaging in horseplay involving spleens or lymph nodes without making a sincere effort to get the other side." So I contacted the USDA's Western Region office, which is located—and let this be a lesson to those who claim that the federal government is poorly managed—in the West.

I spoke with Dr. Bruce Kaplan, a public affairs specialist, who explained that, "on rare occasions," poultry and meat inspectors, as well as plant employees, will become bored and flip meat and poultry organs at each other. (He did not specifically state that these were guys doing this, but some things go without saying.)

"In the poultry plants, they will flip spleens," explained Dr. Kaplan. "In the red-meat plants, they will flip lymph nodes."

Dr. Kaplan stressed that "there is absolutely no danger in terms of food safety." The problem, he said, is the safety of plant workers: "When they walk on the floor where these organs fall, they could slip."

In hopes of making the public more aware of the potential danger. I asked Dr. Kaplan to describe a poultry spleen.

"These are little small spleens," he explained. "They're tiny little slippery spleens."

I think we can draw several conclusions from this story:

1. First and foremost, "Slippery Spleens" would be an excellent name for a rock band.
2. Although it has become fashionable to knock "big government," we must not forget that, without the quick and decisive action by the USDA in the form of acting director Thompson's memorandum, the ordinary public, in the form of food-plant workers, would have no protection from the threat of slipping on organs flipped by USDA inspectors.
3. If the USDA ever has a shortage of inspectors, it should definitely consider recruiting members of Theta Delta Chi.

SPEED TRAP

Recently the federal government, as part of its ongoing effort to become part of the same solar system as the rest of us, decided to eliminate the National Pretend Speed Limit.

As you are aware, for many years the National Pretend Speed Limit was 55 miles per hour (metric equivalent: 378 kilograms per hectare). This limit was established back during the Energy Crisis, when America went through a scary gasoline shortage caused by the fact that for about six straight months, everybody in America spent every waking moment purchasing gasoline. Remember? We all basically went insane. The instant our car's fuel gauge got down to fifteen-sixteenths of a tank, we raced to a service station and spent a couple of hours waiting in line with hundreds of other gasoline-obsessed Americans. It's still a mystery why we did this. Maybe some kind of brain-damaging chemical got in our national water supply, because around the same time everybody also got into disco.

So anyway, the Energy Crisis came to the attention of the federal government, which, swinging into action as only our federal government can, told everybody to get swine-flu shots.

No, wait, that was another crisis. What the federal government did in this particular crisis was declare, in 1974, a National Pretend Speed Limit of 55. This has been strictly observed everywhere except on the actual roads, where the *real* speed limit—the one actually enforced by the police—is a secret, unposted number ranging between 63 and 78, unless an individual police officer does not care for the way you look, in which case the speed limit is zero.

The result is that, for over twenty years, virtually everybody in the United States has been violating the speed limit except for Ralph Nader and elderly people wearing hats. (This system is similar to the one used in foreign countries such as Italy, where the government puts strict-looking speed-limit signs everywhere, but nobody ever sees them because light does not travel fast enough to catch the Italian drivers.)

So finally our government, facing reality, has decided to abolish the National Pretend Speed Limit and let individual states decide how fast drivers can go. The most interesting response so far has come from the extremely rural state of Montana (Official Motto: "Moo"), which announced that there would be *no speed limit* during daylight hours. I was frankly amazed when I read this in the newspaper. I mean, I am not a legal scholar, but to me "no speed limit" means that, theoretically, you can go 400 miles per hour, right?

If that were true, Montana would immediately become an extremely popular destination for your average guy driver on vacation with his family, because guys like to cover a tremendous amount of ground. A guy in Vacation Driving Mode prefers not to stop the car at all except in the case of a bursting appendix, and even then he's likely to say, "Can you hold it a little longer? We're only 157 miles from Leech World!" So if there really were no speed limit, a vacationing guy with the right kind of car—by which I mean

231

"the kind of car that has to be stopped with a parachute"—could cover all of Montana in approximately an hour.

In an effort to check this out, I called Montana, which has an area code and everything, and spoke with Steve Barry, deputy chief of the Montana Highway Patrol.

"Can people drive 400 miles per hour up there?" I asked.

He told me that in all honesty the answer was no. He said that while there was "no theoretical upper speed limit," there was a practical one, determined by police officers in the field, based on factors such as traffic density, road conditions and type of vehicle. So I asked him: What if all the conditions were perfect? What would be the absolute fastest you could legally go? What is the *real* Montana speed limit? Barry answered that, if you pinned him down, his estimate would be around 100 miles per hour.

"At that point," he said, "the majority of the citizens at large would say that's too fast for conditions out here."

So you vacationing guys are going to have to budget *four* hours for Montana. But this is still an improvement, and I'd like to see other areas of the country make a similar effort to have realistic traffic laws. For example, right now the "legal" speed limit in downtown Manhattan is 30. This is absurd. This is the speed limit that Manhattan drivers observe on the *sidewalk*. On the streets of Manhattan, the actual observed speed limits are as follows:

Traveling Uptown or Downtown: 125 miles per hour, unless you have a chance to hit a pedestrian, in which case you may go 150.

Traveling Across Town: Nobody has ever successfully traveled across Manhattan in a motor vehicle.

I'd also like to see speed limits that take into account what song you're listening to on the radio. Ideally, if a police officer pulled you over for doing, say, 95 mph in a 75 zone, and you could prove to him that you were listening to the Isley Brothers' version of "Twist and Shout," he would not only have to let you off, but he would also be required, by law, to sing along with you. It's something for all of us to look forward to as our ever-evolving nation heads toward the twenty-first century, traveling *way* too fast for conditions.

THE HAM
TERRORIST

I hate to put a fly in your ointment, but if you think that
just because you live in America, you are safe from the terror of terrorism, then I have three words for you: ha ha ha.

I make this statement in light of a terrifying incident that
occurred on Christmas Eve, according to an article from the
Newport (Oregon) *News-Times*, written by Gail Kimberling
and sent in by alert reader Deane Bristow, whose name can
be rearranged to spell "Sewer Bandito," although that is not
my central point.

My central point is that, according to this story, a husband and wife were in their home outside of Lincoln City,
which is in Oregon, when the United Parcel Service delivered a package to their house. They were not expecting a
package, and therefore they became convinced (why not?)
that it was a bomb. So, according to the story, the woman
put the package in her car, drove the package to the Oregon
coast, which is also in Oregon, and "heaved it over the cliff"
onto the beach.

The woman then drove to the police station and reported
that there was a bomb on the beach. So far you are probably

laughing. But you will change your tune when you learn what the investigating police officer found. What he found, lying on the beach, was a box containing—bear in mind that this happened in the United States of America, not some foreign country such as the Middle East—a fifteen-pound Virginia smoked ham.

Miraculously, the ham had not detonated, so the officer returned it to the couple, who, according to the article, "very reluctantly opened their front door and accepted it." So luckily this story had a happy ending. But that is no reason for us to break out the celebratory bean dip. Because although in this particular case the package turned out to be an innocent ham, it *could* have been something infinitely more dangerous: It could have been a toilet. Here I am thinking of a story, sent in by many alert readers, from the December 29 *New York Times*, headlined LAWSUIT FILED FOR 2 INJURIES FROM TOILETS. This story, as the headline suggests, concerns a lawsuit filed for two injuries from toilets. These toilets, located in a Bronx condominium, allegedly exploded when they were flushed; the lawyer for the victims is quoted as saying that there is "an epidemic of exploding toilets."

Not that I am bitter, but I've been writing about the exploding-toilet epidemic for years, not to mention the exploding-cow epidemic, the Strawberry-Pop-Tart-combustion epidemic, and the Rollerblade Barbie underpants-ignition epidemic, and have I received any recognition in the form of a large cash journalism award? No, I have been called "sophomoric" and "childish" by various doodyhead critics. But now that the famous *New York Times* has decided to horn in on this story, I suppose it will become "respectable." You're probably going to see presidential-campaign debates wherein all the leading contenders take positions on commodes. Let's just hope that this is not televised.

But the thing to remember is this: If you are at home, and United Parcel Service brings you a toilet that you are not expecting—even one of those nice designer-catalog toilets that have become such popular holiday gifts—do NOT attempt to flush it. Instead, take the simple precaution recommended by law-enforcement authorities such as the FBI and Mel Gibson: Drive the toilet to the Oregon coast and heave it off a cliff. Better safe than sorry!

Of course just because you, as an American, could at any moment be killed by a toilet or a ham, that does not mean that all explosions are bad. As the French say, "au contraire" (literally, "eat my Jockey brand undershorts"). Sometimes, the explosive power of an explosion can be harnessed to benefit humanity, as we learn from various newspaper articles, sent in by many alert readers, concerning the effort last October to move the World War I monument in the city of LaPorte, Indiana.

The monument, a massive piece of granite more than six feet tall, was in a secluded, overgrown location. It was scheduled to be moved to a more prominent place in time for Veterans Day, but efforts to dislodge it from its base with drills and jackhammers had failed. What happened next is not entirely clear, but apparently an unidentified local law-enforcement official contacted an Army Reserve group, which provided some unidentified explosives experts, who used some kind of unidentified explosives to separate the monument from the base. This operation went off without a hitch.

Well, okay, if you want to be picky, there was one teensy

hitch, which was that after the explosion, the monument no longer, in a technical sense, existed. But it definitely was not attached to the base anymore. Mission accomplished!

This story does raise several questions:

- *Who were these "experts"?*
- *How come we never asked them to "move" Saddam Hussein's headquarters?*

But that is water over the dam. The point I want to make, in closing, is that just because things are blowing up all around us in this country, that is no reason for us to cower like rabbits under our beds. We are just as safe in our closets. As Winston Churchill (whose name can be rearranged to spell "Hurls Cow Chin Lint") put it: "We have nothing to fear but fear itself." Of course he was safely over in England at the time.

This is me with President George Bush. During his term in office, he and I often put on rental tuxedos and discussed world events.

I AM NOT A CROOK

Not to toot my own horn, but I'm starting to see a strong voter response to my presidential campaign (Motto: "It's Time We Demanded Less!").

Every day, more and more voters are turning toward me. Granted, they immediately turn away and barf, but that is not the point. The point is that I'm getting attention, and I'm getting it without the negative campaigning and cheap-shot name-calling you're hearing from my dirtbag slimeball opponents.

How strong is my candidacy? Let's take a look at the following chart, which shows, state by state, the developing popular groundswell, as measured by the actual percentages of people voting for me in the early state caucuses and primaries (this chart has a margin of error of three-tenths of an inch):

- *IOWA—Zero*
- *NEW HAMPSHIRE—Zero*
- *DELAWARE—Zero*
- *ARIZONA—Zero*
- *THE PLANET EARTH IN GENERAL—Zero*

I'm sure I don't have to whack you over the head with the significance of these numbers. I'm sure you've already reached the obvious conclusion. "Hey!" you are thinking. "Dave is getting EXACTLY THE SAME VOTE PERCENTAGE AS COLIN POWELL!"

Calm down: There is no need to think in capital letters. But you are correct: I am currently running dead even, state for state, with the man who has been shown in poll after poll to be the nation's first choice for president.

Why are Colin and I so hugely popular? I can answer that in one simple word: "The Issues." Here is where I stand on them as of 8:35 P.M. yesterday:

Crime—You can call me courageous if you want, but I am against crime. I favor the death penalty for everything, including zoning violations. In the case of really, really bad criminals—especially murderers and whoever is responsible for putting ketchup in those little packets they give you at fast-food restaurants—I support a massive government project to develop a way to bring them back to life after we execute them, so we can execute them *again.*

The Budget Deficit—For far too long, politicians have been "sugar-coating" the truth about the deficit, telling us only what they think we want to hear. Well, I say it's time we acted like grown-ups and "faced the music." If you really want to know who's responsible for the budget deficit, go to a mirror, look yourself straight in the eye, and say: "I'M sure as hell not responsible!" Of COURSE you're not! Neither am I! I was hitting golf balls with O.J. at the time.

Taxes—A lot of my opponents have been going around spouting harebrained "pie-in-the-sky" tax schemes that promise "something for nothing." Well I say it's time for a "reality check." I favor a practical, fiscally sound, two-pronged "flat-tax" system, as follows:

Prong One—Everybody would pay less.

Prong Two—You, personally, would pay nothing.

Unlike my opponents, however, I am not suggesting that there is such a thing as a "free lunch." (Under my administration, you will still have to pay for your lunch, although dinner would be free, unless they serve it with those little ketchup packets, in which case they would have to pay YOU.) I fully realize that if *everybody* paid lower taxes, then the government would not have the money it needs to carry out its vital constitutional function of shutting down every other week. Therefore, to offset my tax break, I am proposing a special tax of $10,000 on everybody who gets:

The "Jennifer Aniston Model" Haircut—Jennifer Aniston, for the benefit of those of you who have just arrived here from the fourteenth century, is an actress on the TV sitcom *Friends*, which is about six ordinary young people who lead ordinary lives doing ordinary things just like you—working, watching TV, dating Julia Roberts, etc. This show is hugely popular, and one result has been that roughly 80 percent of American women have decided to do their hair in the same style as Aniston, often with unfortunate results. It's like the seventies, when millions of women got the Farrah Fawcett model hairstyle, thinking this made them look like Farrah Fawcett, when in fact it made them look like French poodles that had fallen into vats of hydrogen peroxide.

Get real, women! Copying somebody's hairstyle doesn't make you look like that person! If I wore my hair like Brad Pitt, would I suddenly look exactly like Brad Pitt? Of course not! I would look exactly like Mel Gibson! But that is some-

241

thing I have learned to live with. Because I happen to be a realist, which is why I know that I will never be president of this great nation unless I can persuade you, the people, to give me your trust in the form of U.S. currency. I'm going to need a LOT of your trust, because I want to present my Vision for America's Future by means of TV commercials suggesting that my opponents are guilty of, at minimum, molesting livestock. So help me out, voters! Let's all do our part, as patriotic citizens, to make this great nation an even better place in which for me to live. You'd better act now, because there are only so many spaces on the Supreme Court.

And speaking of presidents: It has been brought to my attention that I am a stupid idiot because in a recent column I attributed the statement "We have nothing to fear but fear itself" to Winston Churchill. This statement was of course made by Franklin D. Roosevelt, inventor of the phonograph.

DAVE MEETS THE DEATH TREE

There is a simple explanation for why I wound up dangling from a rope 75 feet in the air over a beaver dam somewhere in Idaho: I was a house guest.

You know how it is, when you're a house guest: If your host suggests an activity, you, as a polite person, tend to say "sure."

My host in this case was my good friend Ridley Pearson, who makes his living writing thriller novels, which means he spends his days thinking up sentences like: "Roger awoke in a dark room and sensed immediately that his body had been surgically removed from his head."

What I'm saying is that Ridley has some spooky closets in the mansion of his mind. This is why I should have been suspicious when, the night I arrived at his house, he casually said, "I thought that tomorrow we could climb a tree."

This struck me as an odd activity for a couple of guys in their forties. Guys our age generally prefer a more mature type of recreation, such as scratching. It was as if Ridley had said, "I thought that tomorrow we could play hide-and-seek." But I was a house guest, so all I said was "sure."

The next morning we had breakfast with Ridley's brother, Brad, and a friend named Amos Galpin, and then the four of us set off in Ridley's car to find a tree to climb. This enabled me to see some of Idaho (official motto: "Nobody Knows Where It Is"). It's a nice state, containing a tremendous quantity of scenery as well as several roads and at least one city named "Ketchum." The state license plate says "IDAHO" on the top, and on the bottom it says—I am not making this up—"FAMOUS POTATOES." Apparently this was judged to be the most alluring possible license-plate slogan, narrowly edging out "IDAHO—A WHOLE LOT OF ROCKS" and "IDAHO—YOU'LL SMELL THE COWS."

Most of Idaho is outdoors, the result being that local residents are able to enjoy year-round interaction with the natural environment, which gradually drives them insane. At least that's apparently what happened to Ridley, Brad, and Amos, because they have turned tree-climbing into a serious, full-fledged sport, with special equipment and everything.

They do not climb just any tree. We drove past several million normal, sturdy, vertical trees before stopping at what had to be the most unsafe-looking tree in North America. I could not believe that the tree authorities even permitted this tree to exist. It was next to a beaver pond, and it was leaning WAY over at a stark angle, looking as though it would crash to the ground if a beetle climbed up it, let alone four middle-aged guys who had recently consumed large omelets.

"Is this tree *safe*?" I asked the guys.

"Ha ha!" they reassured me. They then helped me put on the special tree-climbing equipment, which they call a "harness," although what it looks like is an enormous green athletic supporter. It has a pair of ten-foot safety straps attached to it; the idea is that you clip these to the branches as you climb, so that if you fall, instead of smashing into the ground and getting killed, you fall only until your safety strap becomes taut, at which point you turn into a human pendulum and slam into the side of the tree and get killed.

At least that's what I was thinking as I inched higher and higher up the Death Tree. The other guys seemed oblivious to the danger.

"Look at that view!" they'd remark.

"Huh!" I'd reply, admiring the scenic vista of the two square inches of bark directly in front of my face. I hate heights. I was clinging to this tree so passionately that I might very well have committed an act of photosynthesis with it. And it did not help my mood any to know that the area was infested with beavers. At any moment I expected to hear a tail slapping on the water, which is the beaver signal for "COME QUICKLY! DORKS IN GIANT JOCK-STRAPS HAVE CLIMBED AN EASY-TO-GNAW-DOWN TREE!"

But beavers did not gnaw down our tree. What happened was much worse: When we got near the top of the tree, Ridley informed me that we were going to get down by "rappelling," a technique that was invented by mountain climbers who had spent a lot of time at high altitudes with no oxygen getting to their brains.

The way rappelling works is, you close your eyes, jump out of the tree, and slide down on a slim, unsafe-looking rope, which is attached to your harness via a metal fitting that enables you to slide WAY faster than would be possible under the influence of gravity alone, so that you reach speeds estimated at 450 miles per hour as you hurtle toward the ground, crashing through branches while your fellow climbers shout helpful instructions that you cannot hear because you're devoting all of your mental energy to sphincter control. At least that's how I handled it.

All in all, it was an extremely memorable experience that I will devote the rest of my life to trying to forget. I'm looking forward to the day when Ridley is *my* house guest, so that I can plan an equally fun activity for him. I'm thinking maybe we could play tag.

With chain saws.

UP A TREE

When my friend Ridley Pearson invited me back to Idaho, I said to myself: He is NOT getting me up another tree.

I was still combing sap out of my hair from a trip to Idaho last fall, when Ridley talked me into—this is an Idaho sport—climbing way up into a blatantly hostile tree and then getting back to Earth by "rappelling," which means "sliding down at the Speed of Fear on a rope approximately the same width as a strand of No. 8 spaghetti."

I frankly don't know why I let Ridley talk me into anything. He writes thriller novels, which means that he spends most of his time thinking up newer and better ways to murder people. He's always leaving himself little reminder notes with plot ideas like: "Killer is beautician-herpetologist who puts coral snake in hair dryer."

Here's a true story: I was staying at Ridley's house, and we went to the market for groceries, and I was grinding up a bag of coffee when Ridley wandered over. After watching me for a moment, he said: "A murderer could put poison into the grinding machine, so the next person to use it would grind poison into the bottom of his coffee bag. It could be weeks before the poison got into the coffee.

There'd be *no way* to trace it." Then, smiling contentedly, he wandered off to buy cold cuts. My host.

So anyway, when I went back to Idaho, I vowed that Ridley was absolutely not, no way, forget about it, going to get me up in another tree. I saw no reason to risk getting killed by falling. Instead, I elected to risk getting killed by drowning.

Specifically, I went "whitewater rafting" on the Salmon River, which gets its name from the fact that it has virtually no salmon in it. It used to have a lot, but then a bunch of dams got built, which is bad for the salmon, who frankly are not rocket scientists. Despite the fact that they spend most of their lives in the Pacific Ocean, they have decided that the only place they can spawn is smack dab in the middle of Idaho. So every year they try to swim hundreds of miles upstream past all these dams, and only a few make it, and by that point the female salmon have severe headaches, so precious little spawning occurs.

In an effort to correct this situation, the federal government has wildlife rangers trying to help the salmon by roping off the spawning areas, playing Julio Iglesias music underwater, etc. I've been critical of government programs in the past, but as a person concerned about the environment, I have to admit, in all honesty, that the federal salmon effort is stupid. It would make a WHOLE lot more sense to have the rangers fly low over the Pacific Ocean in planes with loudspeakers blaring the announcement: "SPAWN RIGHT HERE, YOU MORONS!" Of course you run the risk that one of the planes would fly over a cruise ship, and the passengers, mistaking the announcement for an order from the captain, would suddenly start engaging in mass carnal behavior right in the buffet line, but that is the price you pay to protect the environment.

Anyway, speaking of vessels, I went whitewater rafting, which is a little scary inasmuch as some idiot—the authorities should look into this—has placed rapids *right in the river.* Fortunately, the rafting company requires you to wear a life jacket, which means that in the event that you get tossed out of the boat, you'll stay safely afloat long enough to freeze to death. The Salmon River is extremely cold, consisting primarily of recently melted snow rushing down from the mountains; this is nature's way of cleansing the slopes of deceased skiers.

But I made it through the rapids okay, and I was starting to think my Idaho trip was going to be casualty-free, when Ridley invited me to spend a night in a "yurt" that he built out in the mountains. I said sure, not realizing that "yurt" is a Mongolian word meaning "small dome-shaped structure that gets so cold at night you would be warmer if you slept in the Salmon River."

But the cold was not the problem. The problem was that (1) my son, Rob, was with me, and (2) there were trees near the yurt. Rob is fourteen, so naturally he wanted to engage in the most life-threatening possible activity, and here's what the ever-obliging Ridley came up with: He strung a rope between two trees, at an altitude of approximately 150,000 feet, the plan being to dangle from this rope, on a pulley, and slide from one tree to the other. My feeling was that, if you needed to get from one tree to the other—even a salmon would figure this out—you could just walk. But no, Ridley and Rob had to take the Batman route, and Ridley decided that, when Rob went across the rope, there had to be an adult on each end.

And thus, once again, I found myself way up in an Idaho tree, embracing the trunk with a passion normally associated with Bob Packwood. Fortunately everything worked out: Rob came zipping across on the rope and claimed to enjoy it, although for several hours he remained the color of vanilla yogurt. I finally got back down to Earth and vowed to never again get up on anything higher than a medium-pile carpet. We went back to the yurt and spent a relaxing night watching our breath turn instantly to sleet. The next morning, Ridley made us a hearty breakfast. I made my own coffee.

ONE POTATO, TWO POTATO...

For more than a year now, alert readers have been sending me alarming newspaper articles about the "potato gun," a bazooka-sized device that can shoot a potato several hundred yards at speeds up to 1,000 feet per second. To give you an idea of how fast that is, an ordinary potato, on its own, will rarely travel more than four feet per day, even during the height of mating season.

Potato guns—which have already been banned in some municipalities—can be easily made from plastic pipe available in any plumbing-supply store; the explosive force comes from ordinary hair spray, which is ignited by an electrical spark. Needless to say I will not provide any specific details concerning how to construct these devices, because a great many young people read this column, and they already know how to construct these devices.

Anyway, I recently got a fax from an individual whom I will identify here only as Buzz Fleischman. Buzz, who makes his living performing humor at corporate meetings and other functions, and who by the way currently has some openings on his calendar, informed me that he had constructed a potato gun, and was willing to demonstrate it for the purpose of helping me, as a responsible adult, better understand just how alarming this menace is.

We decided to fire the potato gun from the roof of my place of employment, the *Miami Herald* (motto: "We Are Still Keeping an Eye on Gary Hart"). Let me stress that the *Miami Herald* is a responsible institution that does NOT ordinarily allow people to shoot potatoes from its premises. We were able to do it only because we met the very strict requirement of not asking for permission. It was a Covert Operation, during which we addressed each other only by code names except when we forgot. (For ease of memorization, we both used the code name "Eagle One.")

Once we got up on the *Herald* roof, we decided to fire the potato gun toward Biscayne Bay. Our other option was to fire it toward the city of Miami, which would have been a serious mistake because hundreds of local residents would undoubtedly have fired back (and not with potatoes, either).

To load the gun, Buzz stuffed a potato into the barrel and shoved it down with a pole, then sprayed some Aqua Net Super Hold hair spray into the detonation chamber. He then aimed the gun at the bay and pressed the ignition device, and FWOOOM, the potato came blasting out of the gun and went way way WAAAAY out over the water and landed approximately in Portugal.

As responsible adults, Buzz and I were very alarmed by this demonstration. We shot off a bunch more potatoes to see if we would continue to be alarmed, and we were. We also got excellent results with an onion.

But as any reputable scientist will tell you, the "acid test" of the alarmingness of this type of device is what happens when you shoot a Barbie doll out of it. We used the "Gymnast Barbie" model, which comes with a little gold medal. First we loaded a potato into the gun, then we put Gymnast Barbie into the end of the barrel, with just her head and hairstyle sticking out. Then we pointed the potato gun straight up and FWOOOM up went Barbie, high in the sky, smiling perkily, waving her arms and legs gymnastically around inside a cloud of potato atoms before finally landing in a really unladylike pose.

Needless to say these results were extremely alarming. Because if the potato gun can be used to shoot Barbie dolls, then it is only a matter of time before some fiendish criminal mind thinks of using one to shoot a Kellogg's Strawberry Pop-Tart. So we tried that, too. It was pretty disappointing. The gun made a noise like "phoo" and spat Pop-Tart fragments a short, non-alarming distance.

Nevertheless as concerned adults we all need to become wrought up about this menace. People should form organizations and write angry letters. Congress should hold hearings. The Clinton administration should announce a definite policy and then change it. Maybe the Warren Commission should get back together. Also the Defense Department should probably go on Red Alert, because any day now Portugal is going to start shooting back.

THE EVIL EYE

*C*all me a wild and crazy guy if you want, but recently, on a whim, I decided to—why not?—turn forty-eight.

It's not so bad. Physically, the only serious problem I've noticed is that I can no longer read anything printed in letters smaller than Shaquille O'Neal. Also, to read a document, I have to hold it far from my face; more and more, I find myself holding documents—this is awkward on airplanes—with my feet. I can no longer read restaurant menus, so I fake it when the waiter comes around.

> **Me (pointing randomly):** *I'll have this.*
> **Waiter:** *You'll have your napkin?*
> **Me:** *I want that medium rare.*

It's gotten so bad that I can't even read the words I'm typing into my computer right now. If my fingers were in a prankish mood, they could type an embarrassing message right in the middle of this sentence HE'S ALWAYS PUTTING US IN HIS NOSE and there is no way I'd be able to tell.

I suppose I should go see an eye doctor, but if you're forty-eight, whenever you go to see any kind of doctor, he or she invariably decides to insert a lengthy medical item into your body until the far end of it reaches a different area code. Also, I am frankly fearful that the eye doctor will want me to wear reading glasses. I have a psychological hang-up about this, caused by the fact that, growing up, I wore eyeglasses for 70,000 years. And these were not just any eyeglasses: These were the El Dork-O model, the ones that come from the factory pre-broken with the white tape already wrapped around the nose part. As an adolescent, I was convinced that my glasses were one of the key reasons why the opposite sex did not find me attractive, the other key reason being that I did not reach puberty until approximately age thirty-five.

Anyway, other than being functionally blind at close range, I remain in superb physical condition for a man of my age who can no longer fit into any of his pants. I have definitely been gaining some weight in the midriff region, despite a rigorous diet regimen of drinking absolutely no beer whatsoever after I pass out. The only lower-body garments I own that still fit me comfortably are towels, which I find myself wearing in more and more social settings. I'm thinking of getting a black one for funerals.

Because of my midriff situation I was very pleased to read recently about the new Miracle Breakthrough Weight Loss Plan for Mice. In case you missed this, what happened was, scientists extracted a certain chemical ingredient found in thin mice, then injected it into fat mice; the fat mice lost 90 percent more weight than a control group of fat mice who were exposed only to Richard Simmons. The good news is that this same ingredient could produce dramatic weight loss in human beings; the bad news is that before it becomes available, it must be approved by the Food and Drug Administration (motto: "We Haven't Even Approved Our Motto Yet"). So it's going to take a while. If you're overweight and desperate to try this miracle ingredient right away, my advice to you, as a medical professional, is to get hold of a thin mouse and eat it. It can't be any worse than tofu.

But getting back to aging: Aside from the vision thing, and the weight thing, and the need to take an afternoon nap almost immediately after I wake up, and the fact that random hairs—I'm talking about *long* hairs, the kind normally associated with Cher—occasionally erupt from deep inside my ears—aside from these minor problems, I am a superb physical specimen easily mistaken for Brad Pitt.

Not only that, but I have the mind of a steel trap. Of course very few things in the world—and I include the Home Shopping Network in this statement—are as stupid as a steel trap. What I'm saying is, I have definitely detected a decline in some of my mental facilities. For example, the other day I was in my office, trying to perform a fundamental journalistic function, namely, fill out an expense report, and I needed to divide 3 into a number that, if I recall correctly (which I don't; that's the problem), was $125.85, and *I couldn't remember how to do long division.* I knew I was supposed to put the 3 into the 12, then bring something down, but what? And how far down? And would I need the "cosine"?

I was starting to panic, when all of a sudden—this is why you youngsters should pay attention in math class—my old training came back to me, and I knew exactly what to do: Ask Doris. Doris works in my office, and she has a calculator. I guess I should start carrying one around, along with some kind of device that remembers (a) people's names,

(b) where I put the remote control, and (c) what I had planned to do once I got into the kitchen other than stand around wearing a vacant expression normally associated with fish.

But so what if my memory isn't what it used to be? My other mental skills are as sharp as ever, and I'm confident that I can continue to do the kind of astute analysis and in-depth research that have characterized this column over the years, which is why today I want to assure you, the readers, that my advancing age will in no way change the fact that MAINLY HE SCRATCHES HIMSELF.

CONFLICT MANAGEMENT

Today's Topic for Married People Is:
Coping with Anger

E ven so-called perfect couples experience conflict. Take Canada geese. They mate for life, so people just assume they get along well; when people see a goose couple flying overhead, honking, they say, "Oh, that's SO romantic." What these people don't realize is that honking is how geese argue. ("Are you SURE we're heading north?" "YES, dammit." "Well I think we should ask somebody.") The only reason they mate for life is that they can't afford lawyers.

It's the same with humans. Even if you love somebody very much, you eventually discover that this person has irritating habits, such as leaving toenail clippings around the house as though they were little art displays; or not disposing of the potato-chip bag after eating everything in it except three salt molecules at the bottom; or secretly being also married to somebody else; or humming the song "A Horse with No Name"; or responding to every single statement you make—including obviously factual ones, such as that Montpelier is the capital of Vermont—by saying "Well, that's *your* opinion."

No matter how much you love your spouse, eventually the smooth unblemished surface of your relationship will be marred by a small pimple of anger, which, if ignored, can grow into a major festering zit of rage that will explode and spew forth a really disgusting metaphor that I do not wish to pursue any further here. This is why you married couples need to learn to cope with your anger, unless you are Roseanne and Tom Arnold, in which case you need to move to separate continents and shut up.

For an excellent example of a married couple coping with anger, we turn now to an incident that occurred several years ago involving my brother, Sam, and his wife, Pat, when they were on a long car trip. After many hours on the road, they reached Charleston, South Carolina, where they were going to visit an old family friend. Pat was driving, and Sam was giving directions, and they got into an argument about the way he was giving them. (If you don't understand how such a petty issue could cause an argument, then you have never had a spouse.)

So Pat decided, okay, if Sam was so good at directions, then HE could drive the stupid car. She got out, slammed the front door, and opened the back door to get in the back with their two-year-old son, Daniel. And then she decided, hey, why should she ride in the back, like a child? So she slammed the back door. But before she could open the front door, Sam, assuming she was in the car, drove off. Pat was left standing, all alone, at night, with no money, wearing a T-shirt, and a miniskirt, in what turned out to be a very bad neighborhood.

"Hey, pretty lady!" called a male voice.

Meanwhile, in the car, Sam was driving with great intensity and focus, reading street signs, making left turns and right turns, showing Pat (he thought) just how excellent his directions were. It was not until he had gone a considerable distance that he realized Pat was being very quiet.

"Pat?" he said.

Silence.

"Daniel," said Sam, trying to sound as calm as possible, "is Mommy back there?"

"No," said Daniel.

"Okay, Daniel," said Sam, performing a high-speed turn. "Just be calm." He immediately became lost.

Meanwhile, back in the bad neighborhood, Pat, walking briskly away from various admiring males, found a bus station with a pay phone, called 911, and explained where she was.

"Do NOT go outside," said the 911 person.

Meanwhile Sam, driving frantically while reminding Daniel to stay calm, had located the general area where he'd left Pat. He saw a police officer, rushed up, and quickly told him what had happened.

The officer said: "You left your wife HERE?" Without another word, the officer leaped into his patrol car and, tires squealing, roared off. Sam never saw him again.

Meanwhile, at the bus station, another officer, sent by the 911 person, had found Pat, who was explaining the situation.

"My husband and I were having a disagreement," she said, "and . . ."

"Oh," said the officer. "A domestic."

"No," said Pat. "It's *not* a domestic. My husband just . . ."

Another officer arrived.

"Hey," said the first officer. "I got a domestic here."

"It's NOT a domestic," said Pat.

Pat was taken to the police station, where the officer called the old family friend—this being the only person Pat knew in Charleston—and explained the situation.

"I got a Pat Barry here on a domestic," he said.

"IT'S NOT A DOMESTIC," said Pat, in the background.

Fortunately, Sam also called the old family friend, and he and Pat were reunited at the police station, where Pat graciously elected not to seek the death penalty. So everything worked out fine except that to this day Daniel becomes mildly concerned when Mommy gets out of the car.

Anyway, I hope Pat and Sam's experience serves as a lesson to you spouses about the importance of not letting your anger fester, and of using proven psychological techniques for dealing with conflict in your marriage. For example, on long car trips, one of you should ride in the trunk.

MR. DAVE'S
BEAUTY TIPS

Today's Topic Is: Your Hairstyle

Is your hairstyle important? To answer that question, let's consider the starkly different career paths of two individuals: Albert Einstein and Tori Spelling.

Tori Spelling is a top celebrity and highly successful television star, despite having the natural acting prowess of a Salad Shooter. Why? Because she always has a neat, modern hairstyle. Also her father produces every show on television except the test pattern. But her hair is surely a factor.

In contrast, Albert Einstein—despite being a brilliant genius who not only discovered the Theory of Relativity ("$E=H_2O$") but also prepared his own tax returns—never so much as appeared on *Hollywood Squares*. He auditioned repeatedly, but the talent coordinators always turned him down.

"What was that on his head?" they'd ask each other after he left the studio. "A yak?"

So we see that hairstyle is very important. This is true

even in the animal kingdom. Baboons, for example, spend countless hours grooming each other, applying conditioners, combing fur over the bald spots on their butts, and using all the other little styling tricks that make them the confident, successful, and cosmopolitan creatures that they are, equally at home on a rotting zebra carcass as on a rotting giraffe carcass.

It is no different with humans. If you have a lunch meeting with an important potential business client, you are definitely going to make a strong impression if you reach over and pick a live insect out of his or her hair. But it also helps if you have a nice hairstyle. Unfortunately, a lot of people—and here I am thinking of women—hate their own hair. In my experience, when a woman looks at herself in a mirror, even if her hairstyle is really nice, she sees Chewbacca.

Men, on the other hand, tend to feel positive about their hair. Even if a man has a grand total of only four hairs left, he will grow them to the length of extension cords and carefully arrange them so they are running exactly parallel, two inches apart, across his otherwise stark naked skull, and he will look at himself and think, "Whoa, these four hairs are looking GOOD."

But whether you're a woman or a man, you should know the basics of hairstyle management, as presented here in the popular Q and A formal:

Q. *How can I have really nice hair?*
A. *If you look at the models in commercials for hair-care products, you'll notice that their hair is thick, glossy, lustrous, and manageable. What's their secret? It's simple: They were born with nice hair. That's why they are pro-*

fessional hair models, whereas you and the late Albert Einstein are not.

Q. **Should balding white men shave their heads, the way many African-American men, such as Michael Jordan, do?**

A. *No. It's not fair, but the simple truth is that balding African-American men look cool when they shave their heads, whereas balding white men look like giant thumbs.*

Q. **Why is it that some older women, when their hair starts to turn gray, instead of dyeing it back to whatever natural-looking shade it originally was, decide to dye it roofing-tar black or traffic-cone orange, which are colors normally associated with Halloween?**

A. *Apparently it is some kind of sorority initiation.*

Q. **What is the best way to style my hair?**

A. *You are asking the wrong person. I've been trying for over forty years, with absolutely no success, to get my hair to form a simple part. All I want is a basic straight line, such as can be found on Al Gore, the vice president, and Ken, the doll. So every morning, right after my shower, I attempt to style my hair with a brush and a hair dryer. I cannot begin to tell you how hilarious my hair thinks this is. You've heard of "free-range" chicken, right? Well, I have "free-range" hair. It laughs gaily and dances in the blow-dryer breeze, humming "Born Free." When I'm done, it looks* exactly *the same as when I started. It is no closer to forming a part than Dom DeLuise is to winning the Olympic pole vault.*

Q. **When you were in New York on a book tour several years ago, did you briefly find yourself in the same television-studio makeup room as Barbara Walters?**

A. Yes.

Q. What is her styling secret?

A. Enough hair spray to immobilize a buffalo.

Q. Speaking of famous celebrities, did Madonna discuss any hair-related issues in her diary as published in the November issue of Vanity Fair?

A. Yes. On page 224, Madonna had this to say about acting in the movies: "People sit around all day scrutinizing you, turning you from left to right, whispering behind the camera, cutting your nose hairs . . ."

Q. Madonna has NOSE HAIRS?

A. You wouldn't believe. Sometimes she requires a machete.

Q. What about Princess Diana?

A. She is known, around the beauty salon, as "Weasel Nostrils."

Q. That would be a good name for a rock band.

A. Yes.

Q. In conclusion, what is the one word that describes the key to a successful hairstyle?

A. "Hat."

STEALING THE SHOW

Today I would like to explain how I became a career criminal. Basically, it was Oprah's fault.

It started when I was on a book tour, which is when you fly all over the place promoting your book, living out of a carry-on suitcase, wearing the same clothes week after week, until you reach the point where they refuse to let you on any more airplanes because your B.O. vapors keep setting off the smoke alarms.

So on day six, or possibly seventy-four, of the tour, the publisher called to tell me that the *Oprah* show had called to ask if I wanted to be on. Of course I said yes. Oprah is, by far, the most powerful force in the book industry; when she endorses a book, millions of loyal viewers rush right out and buy it. If Oprah were to mention that she's reading the factory repair manual for the 1957 model Hotpoint toaster, it would immediately become the No. 1 bestseller in the world.

So virtually all authors—and I include Herman Melville in this statement—will do virtually anything to get on *Oprah*. We are total sluts about this. If the *Oprah* people decided to do a show on the topic "Authors with Fruit in Their Ears," you'd tune in to *Oprah* and see top literary figures such as Norman Mailer and Joyce Carol Oates sitting there with bananas jutting out of both sides of their heads, going "WHAT? WHAT?"

So I was more than willing to go on the show. The problem was that the topic of my book, which is computers, had nothing to do with the topic of the show I was going to be on, which was "Things We Do in Secret." As the producer explained to me, the idea for the show was that people would confess to bad things that they had done, such as borrowing something and never returning it. The producer wanted to know if I was willing to confess to something; the clear implication was that if I wasn't, I might not be on the show.

So I said heck yes, sure, you bet, I would be THRILLED to confess to something. I would have claimed full responsibility for the Kennedy assassination, if necessary.

The crime I finally came up with, however, was hotel theft. The specific incident occurred some years ago when I was staying in a luxury Hyatt hotel. There was a little plastic sign in the bathroom that said: "Our towels are 100 percent cotton. Should you wish to purchase a set, they are available in the gift store. Should you prefer the set in your bathroom, a $75 charge will automatically be added to your bill."

This was Hyatt's polite way of saying, "If you steal our towels, we'll charge you 75 bucks."

So I stole the sign.

Really. I kept it in my guest bathroom for a couple of years, to amuse guests. When I told the *Oprah* producer about this, she decided it was perfect, but there was a problem: She said it was "essential" that I bring the sign to the show, so I could deposit it, on the air, in a big "give-back" crate, where they'd be collecting all the stuff that people had stolen. Unfortunately, I was in St. Louis on a book tour, and the sign was back in my guest bathroom in Miami.

So I called my fiancée, Michelle, and asked her to send the sign, via Federal Express, to the *Oprah* show in Chicago. But with only one day to go, I was desperately afraid that the sign wouldn't get there on time, and at the last minute they'd cancel my appearance and put on some diet-book author who had confessed to the O.J. slayings, and my big chance would be gone forever.

I spent several anxious hours sitting in my St. Louis hotel room, fretting about this. And then, suddenly, a thought struck me: *The hotel was a Hyatt.* So I looked around, and sure enough, there was a little plastic sign, very similar to the one I'd stolen. It was actually a no-smoking sign, but I figured that the TV viewers would never know the difference.

So I stole it.

So at this point, I had stolen a SECOND hotel sign, plus I was planning to lie on the air, all so I could get on an *Oprah* show that was supposed to be about confessing your sins.

As it turned out, when I got to Chicago, the first sign had arrived, and I was able to deposit it in the "give-back" crate. Also I had a nice chat with Oprah, who is—and this is my honest, candid assessment, in no way influenced by any hope that she will have me back on her show—the most perfect human being in world history.

So everything worked out for the best, except I still have a stolen Hyatt "no-smoking" sign. My concern is that the Hotel Theft Police will brand me as a repeat offender and throw me into Hotel Prison, where there's nothing to eat but pillow chocolates and you never get any sleep because every ten minutes somebody knocks on your cell door and yells "HOUSEKEEPING!"

Actually, that sounds a lot like a book tour.

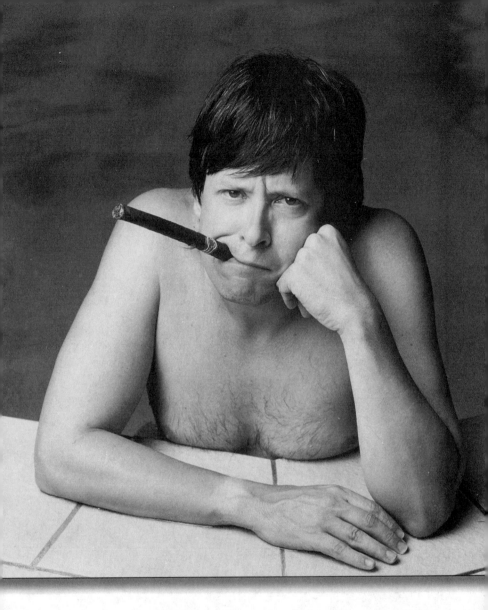

This is a publicity photo taken by a professional photographer. Professional photographers always make me do wacky stuff like get into a cold pool (which I hate) with a cigar (which I hate); this shows everybody how wacky I am. It's undignified and demeaning, but I do it, because the only other option would be to get a real job.